POWDER

Patrick Thorne

POWDER
The Top 50 Ski Runs on the Planet

Quercus

Contents

GREENLAND

BAFFIN
BAY

12

7

HUDSON
BAY

8 9 10

11

4

5

NORTH
AMERICA

2

6

1

ATLANTIC
OCEAN

3

LATIN
AMERICA

SOUTH
AMERICA

47

48

For Europe see next page

GREENLAND SEA

SCANDINAVIA

RUSSIA

EUROPE

BLACK SEA

CASPIAN SEA

RED SEA

AFRICA

INDIA

INDIAN OCEAN

PACIFIC OCEAN

AUSTRALIA

Europe

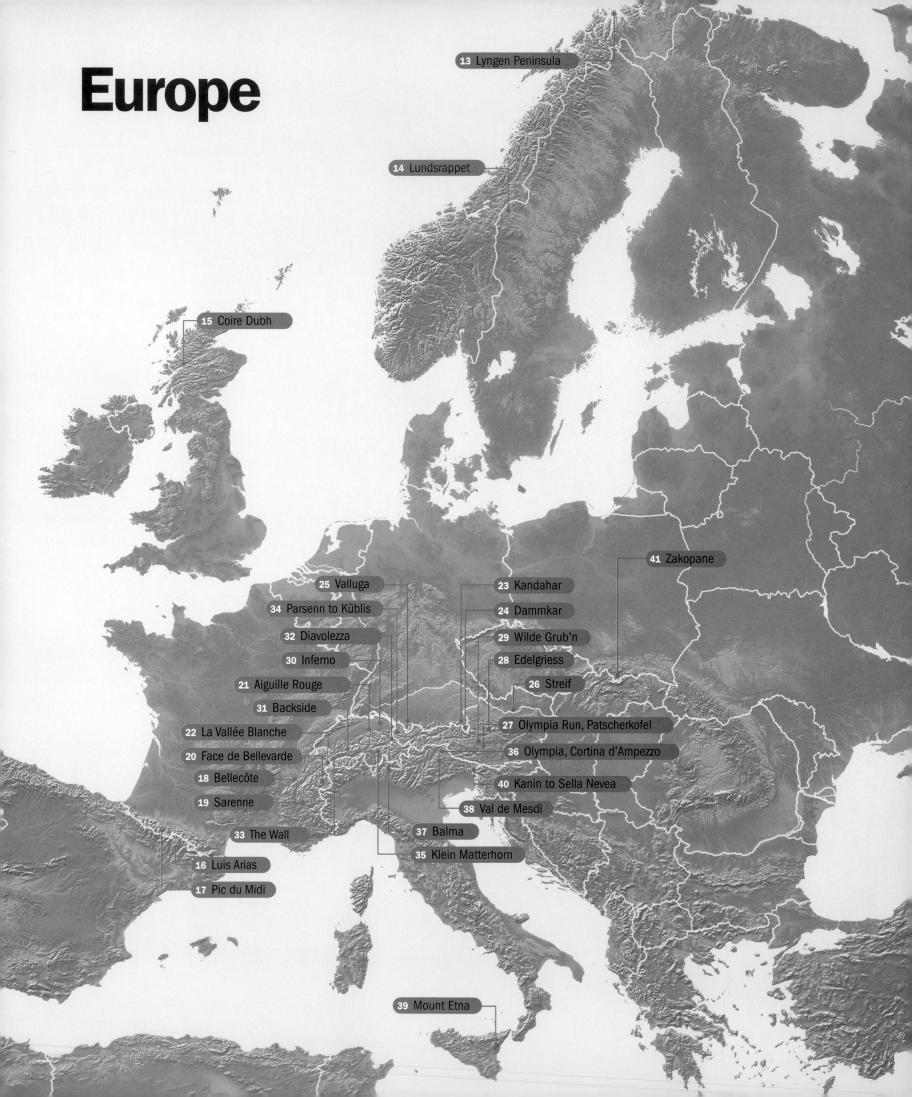

13 Lyngen Peninsula

14 Lundsrappet

15 Coire Dubh

41 Zakopane

25 Valluga

23 Kandahar

34 Parsenn to Küblis

24 Dammkar

32 Diavolezza

29 Wilde Grub'n

30 Inferno

28 Edelgriess

21 Aiguille Rouge

26 Streif

31 Backside

22 La Vallée Blanche

27 Olympia Run, Patscherkofel

20 Face de Bellevarde

36 Olympia, Cortina d'Ampezzo

18 Bellecôte

40 Kanin to Sella Nevea

19 Sarenne

33 The Wall

38 Val de Mesdì

16 Luis Arias

37 Balma

17 Pic du Midi

35 Klein Matterhorn

39 Mount Etna

Introduction

A near-vertical drop or a gentle cruise, virgin powder or well groomed, long, and sustained or fast and furious—everyone has their own idea of what makes the best ski run for them. In any après-ski bar the world over, you'll hear the same debate: "Which are the best ski runs in the world?"

This is, of course, a never-ending discussion and opinions will always vary. With more than 5,000 ski resorts in 80 countries worldwide, and many more virgin slopes to hike up or perhaps take a helicopter to, no one would ever have the chance to ski them all to make a judgment anyway.

But there are some runs that just keep coming up in that après-ski bar conversation—descents that have become the stuff of legend, runs that appear on any skier or snowboarder's bucket list.

The names of many of these runs—the Vallée Blanche, the Hahnenkamm—are well known, sometimes for their magnificent isolation or spectacular views as much as their skiing satisfaction; more often we recognize the names of resorts that are known to include great runs, but not the runs themselves. Whistler and Niseko are well known, for instance, but their most exciting runs are largely not.

Then there are certain select runs in remote locations around the world, known only to a lucky few who would certainly count them among their personal favorites.

Some of these descents have now been skied for more than a century and you ski or board down them in the tracks of some of the most famous names in skiing history. Others are very new, first skied in only the past year or two. But in all these cases, often little is really known of the runs themselves, beyond their name.

In this book we are not attempting to give you that ultimate list, but there are around 50 famous or downright notorious ski runs in the world that most passionate skiers and boarders can agree on, and this is our starting point.

Understanding the maps

In a detailed fact box, each run is summed up with all the essential facts as well as the locator map below. This shows the clearly marked-out run, as well as nearby lifts and cable cars, should there be any.

IN SHORT: The essence of the run in a short summary

TOUGHNESS: How tough it is on a scale of ☠ to ☠☠☠☠☠

FEAR FACTOR: How scary it is on a scale of ☠ to ☠☠☠☠☠

VERTICAL: Vertical drop from start to finish

AVERAGE TIME: Time taken from start to finish at average speed

LENGTH OF RUN: Distance from start to finish

ACCESS: The lift combinations you need to get to the start

BEST TIME: Time of year when conditions are optimal

AVALANCHE KIT: Whether specific avalanche equipment is required

ALTITUDE RANGE: Start and finish altitude of the run

SKIABLE AREA: Area of all runs in the region combined

RUNS: The number of runs in the area

LIFTS: The number of lifts in the area

WEB: Useful websites

GETTING THERE: The nearest airports

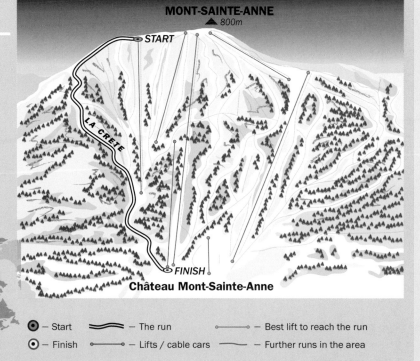

◉ – Start   〰〰 – The run   •—• – Best lift to reach the run
◉ – Finish   •—• – Lifts / cable cars   —— – Further runs in the area

ABOVE: Wilde Grub'n, in the Stubai ski area, is one of Austria's longest ski routes, and especially enjoyable after a fresh dump of powder.

Foreword

S kiing is, quite simply, the best sport in the world. With skis, you're able to explore incredible terrain in some of the most spectacular scenery on Earth. Skiing is speed, instinct, anticipation, and excitement all rolled into one—and if you are born on skis, like I was, you are soon able to ski faster and on steeper terrain than others—which means that you start pushing the sport to its limits. I grew up in Kitzbühel, Austria, right at the bottom of Hahnenkamm, and as a result I find it hard to look at snowy mountains without considering different—and often steep and scary—lines off those mountains. I started skiing at home and was soon traveling around the globe. Downhill, powder, speed ski, ski cross, big mountain ... I loved it all. Before too long, I found myself among the best skiers in the world without realizing how I got there.

Skiing has always been my biggest passion and I am always looking for new projects. I like to ski mountains that no one has dared to ski before, and have made movies documenting my adventures. Even if it looks too scary and crazy for the vast majority, I feel like I know where my limits are. First descents are like climbing without a rope—a crash can be fatal and the thrill is to control your movements to perfection. You also, of course, get to experience the best feeling in the world by gliding down a big mountain—and sometimes being the first person ever to do so. I've never claimed to be the best extreme skier in the world, but I do think I have the most fun on skis of anybody I know.

This book offers a glimpse into that world and guides you through the world's 50 most extreme—yet still accessible—runs for those readers who are accomplished enough skiers to attempt them.

I look back at my lifetime of skiing and sometimes wonder how I did some of it. There is not much I regret, but these days I realize that you'd have to be 25 years old and invincible to even attempt some projects. I take it easier these days, but I will always love the sport.

Go skiing with passion and you will be rewarded with even more passion. Skiing makes me feel alive—and if it does the same to you, then you will always enjoy this magnificent sport.

Axel Naglich

January 2014
Kitzbühel, Austria

North America

McConkey's
Squaw Valley, California, USA
8,997ft (2,743m)

Founded by Alex Cushing in 1949 and run by his family for more than 60 years, Squaw Valley is one of those very few resorts of the thousands around the world that has built a reputation that no amount of money could buy today. Cushing secured the 1960 Winter Olympic Games for his fledgling resort, with opening and closing ceremonies orchestrated by Walt Disney.

Growing to become one of the largest ski areas in North America, Squaw had the novel approach until quite recently of producing a trail map with no trails marked on it—only lifts. The reasoning behind this was that the entire mountain was open should you wish to ski it—although it might have made writing Squaw's entry in this book rather difficult had they stuck to that policy.

Shane McConkey, along with several other of the planet's greatest skiers and snowboarders, honed his skills on the exceptionally challenging terrain provided by Squaw Valley, so it is only fitting that the Californian extreme snowsports mecca has renamed one of its most taxing descents after him.

In honor of Shane McConkey

Such a philosophy ensured that many of North America's greatest extreme skiers were drawn to Squaw, perhaps more than to any other American resort, putting it up there with Chamonix, Verbier, or St. Anton for global credibility. Among them were Jonny Moseley and the late, great, Canadian-born skier, Shane McConkey.

Both have runs named after them at Squaw, but McConkey, an all-round good guy as well as an amazing skier, is sadly no longer with us. He died in an extreme-sports accident in the Italian Dolomites in spring 2009. Having skied off a cliff wearing a wingsuit, Shane's skis failed to release quickly enough and he did not deploy his backup parachute.

Squaw decided to rename one of the resort's most challenging ski areas, Eagle's Nest (not just named to sound impressive—a family of eagles actually used to roost there), in his honor later that year. As with much of the resort's famously challenging terrain, it's accessed from the KT-22 chairlift and, unlike tough terrain at many ski areas, is relatively close to the resort base, so is less subject to closure due to weather issues.

KT-22 was named by the late Wayne Poulsen, who originally bought the land where Squaw is located in 1931 for a railroad company before teaming up with Alex Cushing, who counted the number of kick turns it took his wife Sandy to ski down it—hence the name.

To reach the area it's a short 15-minute hike, turning left from the top of the chair. Remember to give the McConkey memorial sculpture a pat for luck and due respect, as you pass.

Skiing McConkey's, like most other routes accessible from the KT-22 chairlift, means that you are going to be tackling it in front of a half-critical, half-supportive crowd looking straight at you from the chair as you descend. So be prepared not only to "pinball once or twice," as McConkey himself described the risks, but also for possible catcalls from the lift if your wipeout isn't serious—although equally you'll be rewarded with whoops of congratulation if you ride it beautifully. It's rather like being a gladiator in the Roman Coliseum a few millennia ago, as described by Oliver Reed in the famous movie.

Picking the line

There are several different lines down, with the Center Route—one of the steepest lift-served routes in the world, pitching at up to 60 degrees—generally considered the most challenging (and they're all very challenging). Each line has a descriptive name—The Shoulder, Air To The Right, Ambrosia's Alternative, and Freebird, for example, and the suitability of each on any given day will depend on current snow conditions, of course. Generally McConkey's is at its best after easterly storms have deposited plenty of powder to cover the face and fill big powder pillows to bounce into.

From skier's right, the most distant line from the lift, and one of the most infamous, is The Shoulder, which is usually one of the least skied even after fresh powder. This is not just because of the longer hike, but because those in the know are aware that if the snow is not yet deep enough (and even if it is), you can expose up to 20ft (6m) of rock face with a turn. However, the run levels out a little from its initially vertiginous pitch as it reaches the trees and it is one of the more forgiving lines if you do fall.

The Shoulder, as with most of the other lines here, deserves a listing in IMDb (the Internet Movie Database), as it has appeared in countless ski movies, including *Extreme Skiing* and *Licensed to Thrill*. We are in the Hollywood state, after all.

The Center Route is, for most, the most challenging simply due to its pitch (it's also one of the most visible for onlookers), which averages out at around 60 degrees but can increase if a cornice builds through the season at the top, making it potentially as steep as 65 degrees. If that cornice is there, it's important to be careful not to fall through it when picking your line, as has happened in the past. The route is marked by a small pine tree and involves riding down that very steep slope and one or two jumps of 23–33ft (7–10m), depending on the line you take.

LEFT: It's not unusual for several feet of snow to fall in several days on Squaw's slopes, giving superb powder conditions.
RIGHT: An efficient lift system means access to Squaw's steeps is relatively effortless.

For the most extreme only

The other lines are all very alarming for the nonexpert extreme skier in their own way. High Line is considered the most technically challenging, where the slightest error can cause problems; Freebird involves a drop of some 6.6ft (20m) from a starting slope pitching at 68 degrees; while Air To The Right is so named because it involves a jump of around 26ft/8m)—but as the slope is still pitching at 50 degrees when you land, and some very big trees fly toward you, some nifty turning is quickly required.

If all this sounds rather too much—and for all but the most experienced, it definitely is—Squaw is chock-full of iconic terrain that the rest of us can tackle.

Famous runs include the Women's Olympic Downhill—also accessed from KT-22 but without the hike, the Men's Olympic Downhill which runs from Palisades to Siberia, and West Face, renamed Moseley's in February 1998 in honor of Squaw Valley Freestyle Team member and Nagano gold medallist, Jonny Moseley. It is regarded as the best of KT's double-diamond terrain.

Fact file McConkey's

IN SHORT: If you're up to it and prepared to push your limits, this is a run you should aim to do at least once in your life

TOUGHNESS: ☠☠☠☠☠

FEAR FACTOR: ☠☠☠☠

VERTICAL:
8,197–6,199ft
(2,499–1,890m)
(1,998ft/609m vertical)

AVERAGE TIME:
Five minutes

LENGTH OF RUN:
0.93 miles/1.5km

ACCESS:
KT-22 chairlift
then hike

BEST TIME:
December–April

ALTITUDE RANGE:
6,199–8,200ft
(1,890–2,500m)

SKIABLE AREA:
4,000 acres

RUNS: 170

LIFTS: 33

WEB:
squaw.com

GETTING THERE:
Reno Tahoe
International Airport
(41.5 miles/67km),
San Francisco
International Airport
(194 miles/313km) via
all-weather Interstate 80

USA

KT-22
2,500m ▲
START

McCONKEY'S

FINISH

Squaw Valley Base Area

Gunbarrel
Heavenly, California, USA
10,063ft (3,068m)

Do you like moguls? Do you have legs of steel? Are you just slightly insane? Then Heavenly's famous mogul run, The Gunbarrel, is for you.

Gunbarrel is arguably the world's best-known bumps run, plummeting 2,001 vertical feet (610m) of continuous moguls down The Face, the mountainside above Heavenly's California Base Lodge. The fall line is fairly constant and it is basically a case of "bend ze knees" and go. And go. And go. The main variable is the size of the moguls and/or the quality of the snow, which we will discuss a little later.

The one constant, as from most of Heavenly's slopes, is the great views out over Lake Tahoe, which dominates the skyline, stretching 22 miles to the north. At 1,643ft (501m) it is the tenth-deepest freshwater lake in the world, it is 99.9 percent pure and looks awesome.

Just how hard going Gunbarrel is when you visit depends a good deal on your timing. The run, which has played host to the US Freestyle Championships, is normally only groomed once at the start of the season, the day after which the run is, briefly, a great high-speed, steep cruiser. But as more people ski it and the season progresses, those moguls grow and grow.

The steepest run in western North America

Fresh snow—which falls in abundance here—can make the slope still more challenging. By the time spring rolls in, Gunbarrel's location at the bottom of the ski slopes, right above the resort's California base, can mean the snow gets sticky after lunch—adding to that leg burn. The challenge can be greater still, however, on a cold, icy day with little fresh snow as you try to hold an edge on the downside of those moguls on the steep slope. It's worth noting, too, that Gunbarrel is probably the steepest run in western North America with snowmaking. This means it is normally open all season long, not relying on an accumulation of natural snow until it can be skied—although there's normally plenty of it, with Heavenly averaging a world-class 39ft (12m) of powder per season.

Keep in mind that, along with folk looking up at you from the base, Heavenly's iconic red tram soars overhead on the left side of the run, while Gunbarrel's own signature high-speed quad chairlift races up the right side. This enables you to rapidly ascend to try it over and over, but also means that your every move is constantly scrutinized by

RIGHT: You have been warned.

BELOW: The extensive skiing at Heavenly already makes it one of the world's best ski resorts, even before you consider the amazing views of Lake Tahoe spread out below you.

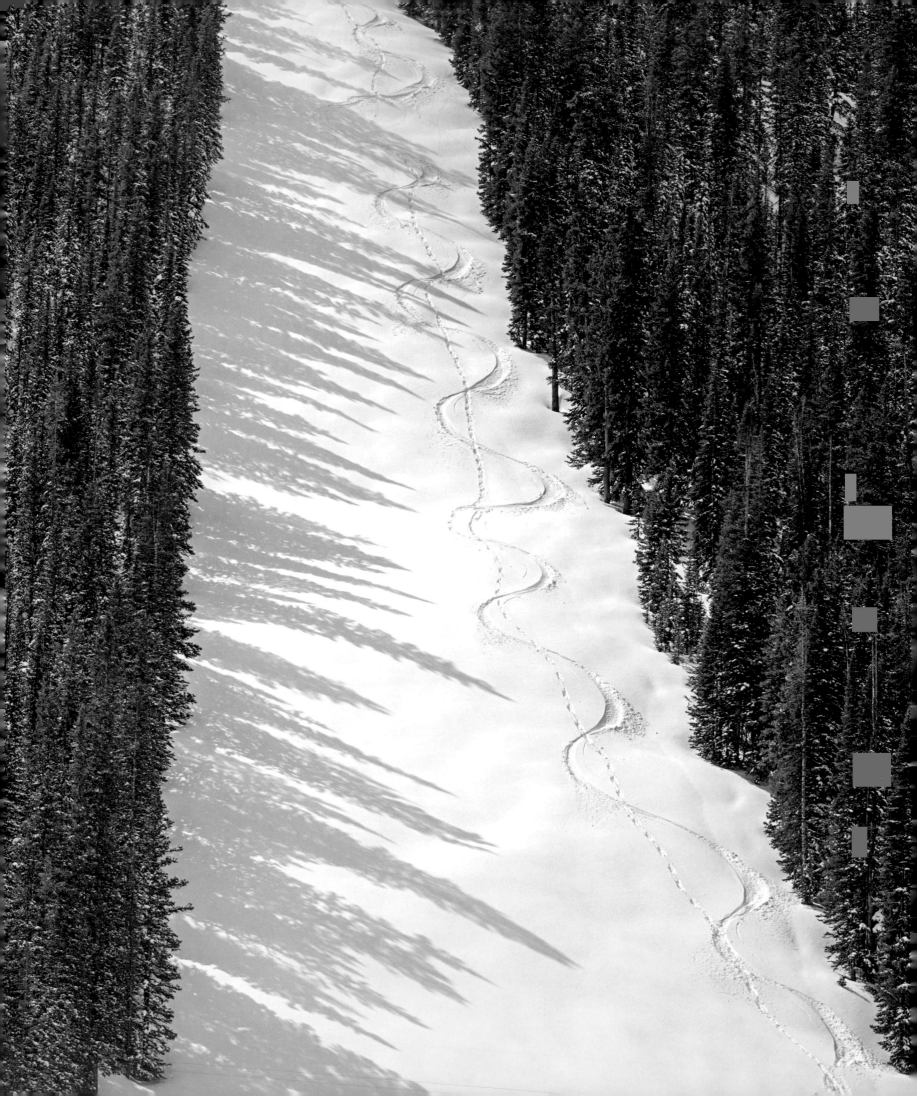

LEFT: Every so often, Gunbarrel gets a white coat of fresh powder and a few folk make fresh tracks before the bumps inevitably reappear.

onlookers—so make sure your bump-bouncing technique is tip-top to avoid embarrassment.

If you do get weary, or just plain embarrassed, you can traverse out into the East Bowl woods, gentler tree skiing to skier's right, or opt for the longer, gentler Round-A-Bout blue-square intermediate trail that crosses The Face rather than going straight down it.

Don't just ski it—Facebook it!

But Gunbarrel is addictive and has even spawned its own "user group" dubbed the Face rats, who do little but ski the run over and over, sometimes clocking up as many as 50 descents—more than 98,400 vertical feet (30,000m) of bumps—in a day. Keeping track of that and comparing your achievements with others got a lot easier a few seasons back when Heavenly's owners, Vail Resorts, launched their high-tech Epic Mix lift tickets. These use a radio-frequency chip in the card that automatically tracks the skier as they move around the slopes, allowing them to check the numbers on their smart phones and post to social media at any time.

Very few runs are associated with one skier, but Gunbarrel will forever be linked to living legend freestyle skier and local Tahoe boy Glen Plake, who has grabbed the world's attention for his multicolored Mohican hairstyle combined with his freestyle skiing prowess from the early 1980s on. The first-ever ski magazine I worked on in London in 1986 featured a young Mr. Plake flying high above a red double-decker London bus.

His contribution to freestyle skiing and to the image of Heavenly led to the resort naming Plake its "Ski.E.O." in 2003 and the following year he was awarded the prestigious Ski Club of Great Britain Centenary Medal, as the august organization celebrated its 100th birthday, "in recognition of his outstanding contribution to and influence upon snowsports."

Although Plake travels the world with his ski career these days, he returns to Tahoe each spring to host the Gunbarrel 25—the challenge being to ski or board Gunbarrel 25 times or more in one day. Well if you like moguls, have legs of steel, and are just slightly insane, what could be better?

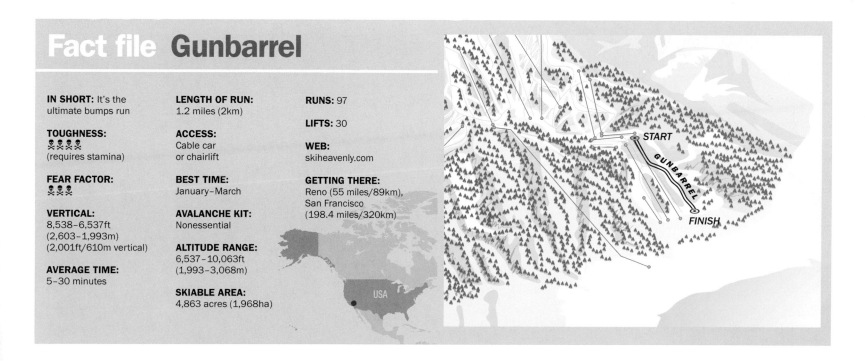

Fact file Gunbarrel

IN SHORT: It's the ultimate bumps run

TOUGHNESS:
☠☠☠☠
(requires stamina)

FEAR FACTOR:
☠☠☠

VERTICAL:
8,538–6,537ft
(2,603–1,993m)
(2,001ft/610m vertical)

AVERAGE TIME:
5–30 minutes

LENGTH OF RUN:
1.2 miles (2km)

ACCESS:
Cable car
or chairlift

BEST TIME:
January–March

AVALANCHE KIT:
Nonessential

ALTITUDE RANGE:
6,537–10,063ft
(1,993–3,068m)

SKIABLE AREA:
4,863 acres (1,968ha)

RUNS: 97

LIFTS: 30

WEB:
skiheavenly.com

GETTING THERE:
Reno (55 miles/89km),
San Francisco
(198.4 miles/320km)

USA

START
GUNBARREL
FINISH

Grizzly
Snowbasin, Utah, USA
9,348ft (2,850m)

Utah famously trademarked the phrase, "The greatest snow on earth" to describe its superlight, fluffy powder which is toasted free of moisture as it arrives over the plains from the Pacific. For once a marketing slogan is pretty accurate, unless you're unlucky when you visit. Better still, there's also an abundance of it (unless you're unlucky when you visit), with several Utah resorts in the world top ten for annual average snowfall tallies of up to 43ft (13m).

But sadly it is not powder freedom for all, as Alta and Deer valleys still ban snowboarders from their slopes, two of only three resorts in the whole of North America (and with most ski areas in Japan that banned borders in the 1980s and '90s now open to all, possibly the whole world) that do.

Not your regular resort

Snowbasin, located in the Wasatch-Cache National Forest, north of Salt Lake City, is, however, a "normal" resort that welcomes all regardless of their race, religion, gender, or snowsports orientation. But in one respect it is not a regular resort, as this was the host of the downhill skiing events at the last Olympics to be held in the US, the 2002 Salt Lake Games.

The resort's Grizzly downhill is one of the longest and steepest on the mountain, taking the entire vertical and, when groomed and iced for racing, one of the most fearsome high-speed descents in the world. The good news is that these days it's generally left as an ungroomed powder run. While Snowbasin's 33ft- (10m-) plus average annual snowfall isn't Utah's greatest, it's still an awful lot of powder.

The terrain where Grizzly was created had been a hike-to, backcountry preserve before it was first lift-accessed in 1998. The course was created from scratch by the great 1972 Olympic downhill gold medallist-turned-piste designer Bernard Russi of Switzerland, who had also shaped the downhill courses for the previous three Olympics. When it was in action for the 2002 Games, the course was compared to the Hahnenkamm by former Austrian and US Olympic coach, Herwig Demschar. It has subsequently been tamed a little with some of the more fearsome sections ironed out, but it remains a great challenge and a great deal of fun.

Named after a local grizzly bear

But although Grizzly is one of the world's newer runs, Snowbasin itself claims to be the oldest continually operated ski area in the US, established

Fact file Grizzly

IN SHORT: Olympic gradient with a lot of Utah powder

TOUGHNESS: ☠☠☠

FEAR FACTOR: ☠☠☠

VERTICAL:
9,348–6,399ft
(2,850–1,951m)
(2,949ft/899m vertical)

AVERAGE TIME:
15 minutes
(Fritz Strobl, Austria:
1:39.13 for Olympic gold)

LENGTH OF RUN:
1.77 miles (2.86km)

ACCESS:
John Paul express quad and after take the Allen Peak tram

BEST TIME:
January–March

AVALANCHE KIT:
Nonessential

ALTITUDE RANGE:
6,399–9,348ft
(1,951–2,850m)

SKIABLE AREA:
3,212 acres (1,300ha)

RUNS: 113

LIFTS: 13

WEB:
snowbasin.com

GETTING THERE:
Salt Lake City
(52 miles/84km)

OGDEN
2,917m

START

GRIZZLY

FINISH

USA

BELOW: Utah's ski slopes have a reputation almost unmatched in the world for their nearly weightless, abundant powder. The slopes of Snowbasin typically receive more than 33ft (10m) of superbly skiable powder each season.

Designed by the best slope designer in the world, skied by the planet's best skiers and home to some of best powder on earth, Snowbasin's terrain ticks all the boxes.

in 1939. It does not feel old when you visit, however: thanks to a major pre-Olympic makeover and subsequent upgrades, there's an excellent mix of state-of-the-art technology and quirky character from the golden age of skiing. US $70 million was spent prior to the games by billionaires Earl and Carol Holding, who have owned Snowbasin since 1984 and are also owners of the famous Sun Valley in Idaho.

The top of the Grizzly run is located on some of Snowbasin's rockiest and steepest terrain on its eastern and northeastern slopes. It begins with an ultrasteep start, Ephraim's Face (named after a grizzly bear once famous in the area), that pitches at 35 degrees. For Olympic racers that means hitting 74 miles (120km) per hour within ten seconds, but with deep powder it instead means a wonderful bouncing descent on the steep fall line.

A double-black-diamond view

Before you take the plunge, as with many of the runs in this book, it's worth taking a minute to take in the scenery from your starting point, more than two miles above sea level, on a sometimes windy precipice. There are views west to the town of Ogden, 17 miles away, and a sweep of the Wasatch Mountains to the east and south. In fact, more unusually, it's worth stopping at the bottom and looking up before you get on the fast quad for the ride up the mountain. Snowbasin is one of those areas that looks especially impressive from below, with a limestone ridge towering above and the steepest terrain up top.

Back at the start of Grizzly, you should also take in the steep double-black-diamond terrain on either side of the course, in particular the Mount Ogden Bowl (on skier's right). This is one of the few sectors of Snowbasin's terrain that's above the treeline, for superb powder bowl skiing on your next lap around. If you follow the ridge toward No Name Peak, you pass the start of the women's downhill course (Wildflower) and then reach some of the steepest descents on the mountain (look for the warning signs), with some excellent long chutes down toward the base.

No guts, no glory

On race day Grizzly is considered a highly technical course of constant turns and drops, with almost no gliding sections where racers can try to regroup and grab a breath. Unlike some modern courses where a relatively unknown racer can win because their team gets the wax right and they can glide to the front, Grizzly is a "no guts, no glory" course, where the strongest and most technically proficient win. In 2002, it was Austria's Fritz Strobl.

Grizzly curves down the mountain, its gradient averaging more than 30 degrees, but with three more supersteep sections such as Flintlock, a third of the way down, which the racers tackled airborne at the Olympics. You may be distracted more by the double-black-diamond glade skiing to your right.

The lower half of the run moves into Offtrack Canyon, named with brilliant simplicity as so many US places are, because a number of trail-grooming tractors have slid off the trail while trying to groom it. You then hit a final steep section, pitching at 37 degrees, into the finish, where you can thank the snow gods that Grizzly is covered in deep, light powder and isn't the sloping ice rink it was on that clear day on February 10, 2002.

Corbet's Couloir
Jackson Hole, Wyoming, USA
10,447ft (3,185m)

Corbet's Couloir requires you to hit the very steep ground running—make that flying—and you won't be able slam on the brakes until the couloir opens up further down.

Fact file Corbet's Couloir

IN SHORT: 3,280 vertical feet (1,000m) of powder and air

TOUGHNESS: ☠☠☠☠ (for experts only)

FEAR FACTOR: ☠☠☠☠☠ (for the fearless)

VERTICAL: 10,211–6,954ft (3,113–2,120m) (3,257ft/993m vertical)

AVERAGE TIME: From 12 minutes

LENGTH OF RUN: 1.9 miles (3km)

ACCESS: The Tram

BEST TIME: Any powder day

AVALANCHE KIT: Nonessential

ALTITUDE RANGE: 6,311–10,447ft (1,924–3,185m)

SKIABLE AREA: 2,533 acres (1,025ha) of in-bounds terrain

RUNS: 116 named runs and trails on the map and another 15

named trails that are not on the map

LIFTS: 12

WEB: jacksonhole.com

GETTING THERE: Jackson Hole (11.8 miles/19km)

USA

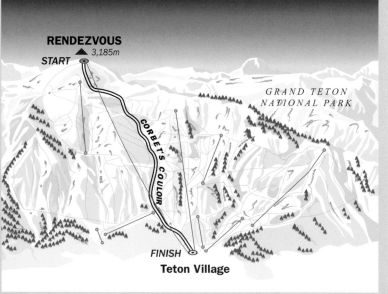

RENDEZVOUS ▲ 3,185m
START

CORBET'S COULOIR

GRAND TETON NATIONAL PARK

FINISH
Teton Village

LEFT: Many of the challenges Jackson Hole has to offer are easily lift-accessed, but some require a short hike in or out.
RIGHT: Jackson Hole is famous for its steep (slopes) and deep (snow), making it a magnet for powder-loving skiers and snowboarders from around the world.

The very name "Jackson Hole" lifts the spirits of any diehard snowsports fan. There are a number of other world-famous resorts, of course, but while Aspen and St. Moritz may bring to mind glitz, or Niseko and Steamboat make you think of light, fluffy powder, Jackson Hole just epitomizes the sheer exhilaration of skiing or boarding in its purest form. Just going for it, because nothing else matters.

Think of famous ski runs at Jackson Hole and the first one to spring to mind is likely to be Corbet's Couloir. It is one of the world's "rites of passage" ski runs although, as it begins with an infamous 10–30-ft (3–9-m) freefall drop-in (depending on your route), onto a slope pitching at more than 50 percent, "ski run" is a rather loose term, for the start at least.

Corbet's is named after one of the original surveyors of the resort, Barry Corbet, who predicted that it would one day be skied when he first saw it in 1963. In fact it was first skied only four years after Mr. Corbet spotted it, by local ski patroler Lonnie Ball in 1967. At first I considered it too obvious a choice for Jackson Hole's greatest run. It may have that infamously scary start, but those who pluck up the courage to jump in nonchalantly report afterward, "skied it, done it," and annoyingly divulge that it's quite easy, actually.

But after considering many of the other great runs at Jackson Hole, the arguments swung back in favor of Corbet's, as long as we add some other elements to our descent to make it all the more enticing. After all, once you have Corbet's out of the way, there's the best part of 3,280 nonstop vertical feet (1,000m) of "top-to-bottom" descent, the longest possible in the USA, including powder bowls, more chutes, and Dick's Ditch, which offers 2,001 vertical feet (610m) of natural bank turns for the highly satisfying lower half of the run. Quite simply, nowhere else can give you this mix and more.

Jump right in

So back to the top and Corbet's Couloir, one of those names in world skiing that every serious skier feels drawn to, along with the Vallée Blanche or the Streif above Kitzbuhel where they run the Hahnenkamm.

Famously, you don't ski into Corbet's—you jump into it. The size of your jump into that gap in the cliffs atop Rendezvous Mountain depends on snow conditions and your route in. In fact, you don't just jump, but (on the most commonly taken approach from skier's left at the top of the couloir) must turn right in the air in order to land successfully. Then a quick turn left once you're on the snow and you've made it, lower limbs intact.

The hard part is actually psyching yourself up to do the jump; once you've landed, the adrenaline rush combined with the joy of skiing the soft powder of Tensleep Bowl are very special. Of course, you could hit the rock face you're trying to avoid with those tight turns, and the vertiginous slope you land on might be hard and icy if there's been little fresh snow. But if it helps you to decide when your natural urge is to bottle out, remember that no one has actually died doing it so far (which can't be said of the Vallée Blanche). And if you do bottle out, as many do, there's an easy way around via Rendezvous Bowl.

Don't look up!

Local experts are divided on the best way to build up to tackling Corbet's. Some say don't look up at it as you ascend in Jackson Hole's famous cable car, as "it looks much worse than it is," while others say that it's best to look and scope your line. In either case, long before you make the tram run from which you plan to do it, it's important to build up to it mentally and physically by trying smaller drops (there are plenty at Jackson Hole) before you go for it. A positive mental attitude can also work wonders—just tell yourself that you can do it, like an American army major stereotype.

But let's not forget those 3,280 or so vertical feet (1,000m). Once you've landed your jump, take the time to enjoy the one-of-a-kind views back up into the couloir and of the famous Jackson Hole cable car. After the powdery Tensleep Bowl below Corbet's, we turn into the double-black-diamond Expert Chutes, which then deposit you out into Toilet Bowl, famous for great snow that piles up thanks to wind on big storm days and having a fun rock to jump off.

Something to write home about

From Toilet Bowl it is a very easy transition and the entire latter half of the descent then follows the black-diamond Dick's Ditch run, a kind of natural halfpipe winding down the mountainside. Dick's Ditch is itself another Jackson Hole favorite, and hosts a strongly contested annual banked slalom race each March.

It's also a gloriously fun way to finish what, for most people, will be the greatest day in their skiing lives, hopefully for all the right reasons. It is one to brag about in the famed Mangy Moose bar at the base of the mountain when each ski day ends, and in ski bars around the world in the years to come.

Walsh's
Aspen, Colorado, USA
11,208ft (3,417m)

Deciding on the best run at Aspen Snowmass is even more tricky than for most of the resorts in this book. Four separate ski areas with some 330 ski runs between them—and that's just the marked terrain. Almost every run type is catered for here, with some spectacular views and one of North America's longest fall lines to (ski) boot.

In the end, a kind of Aspen sampler was decided upon, with a route down Aspen Mountain (or "Ajax" as it's known locally) following the ski-area boundary, which combines two great double-black-diamond runs into one classic top-to-bottom descent.

Before we begin and leap on Aspen's Silver Queen gondola to be whisked straight to the top of our triple-run adventure in one smooth, high-speed ascent, we should look a little at our surroundings.

Aspen was famous before its suitability for winter sports was discovered, first inhabited by the Ute Native North Americans before being settled by prospectors in the 1880s and rapidly rising to be America's biggest silver-mining center. By the early 1890s, a sixth of the nation's and a sixteenth of the world's silver needs were supplied by Aspen's mines. But by the start of the 20th century, the value of silver was in serious decline; Aspen's population fell and its prospects seemed less lustrous.

Then, at the end of the Second World War, the idea of a ski area was mooted. By 1946 what was then the world's longest chairlift was installed and by 1950 Aspen was hosting the Alpine Skiing World Championships, the first ever staged outside Europe.

The rest is history, and an illustrious one, as Aspen rose to be one of the world's greatest resorts, attracting the rich and famous as well as everyone else. They come here partly for the skiing and the scenery, but also because Aspen's modern-day founding fathers sought to create a real community here, with some soul as well as sport, shopping, and glitz. There's a thriving arts scene, featuring music festivals and the like.

Also mirroring those early silver-mining days when hydroelectricity helped power the mines, the Aspen Skiing Company is a global pioneer and strong proponent on environmental issues. So although you may have been responsible for rather a lot of CO_2 in reaching Colorado, at least you know that the resort generates electricity equivalent to its annual usage by harvesting waste methane from a nearby coal mine, thus dramatically reducing emissions that generate greenhouse gasses. Now let's go skiing.

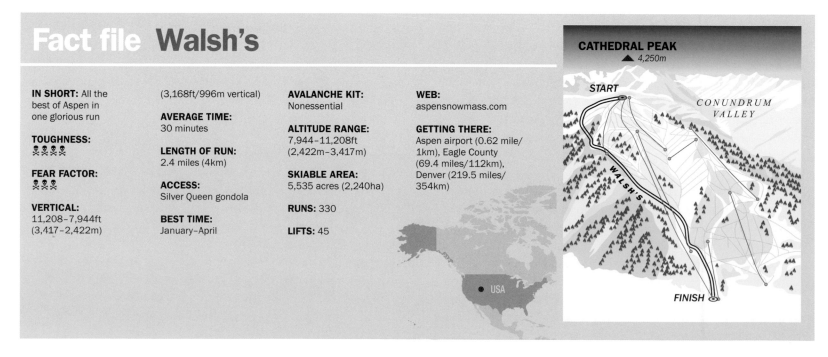

Fact file Walsh's

IN SHORT: All the best of Aspen in one glorious run

TOUGHNESS:
☠☠☠☠

FEAR FACTOR:
☠☠☠

VERTICAL:
11,208–7,944ft
(3,417–2,422m)

(3,168ft/996m vertical)

AVERAGE TIME:
30 minutes

LENGTH OF RUN:
2.4 miles (4km)

ACCESS:
Silver Queen gondola

BEST TIME:
January–April

AVALANCHE KIT:
Nonessential

ALTITUDE RANGE:
7,944–11,208ft
(2,422m–3,417m)

SKIABLE AREA:
5,535 acres (2,240ha)

RUNS: 330

LIFTS: 45

WEB:
aspensnowmass.com

GETTING THERE:
Aspen airport (0.62 mile/
1km), Eagle County
(69.4 miles/112km),
Denver (219.5 miles/
354km)

CATHEDRAL PEAK
▲ 4,250m

START

CONUNDRUM VALLEY

WALSH'S

FINISH

USA

Steep enough for paragliders

Walsh's is one of the three double-black-diamond runs that drop off the east side of Aspen Mountain on a lightly wooded slope. After leaving the gondolas, turn skier's right and simply follow the boundary. An early indication of its steepness is that paragliders launch themselves off the mountain just here, and the run is closed earlier than the rest of the mountain from 3 p.m. each day.

The run may not look much from the top, but don't be fooled—one of the best things about it is the way that it drops off at the breakover, at which point it seems like you are dropping onto the valley floor below. Walsh's is wide enough for you to pick your exposure based on snow conditions. Except for early in the season it is usually bumped up—but since only the best skiers on the hill are skiing it, the bumps are wide apart and have good rhythm.

The slope pitches at an average 35 degrees (but is steeper in places) and from its slopes there are great views up Independence Pass and into parts of the Hunter Frying Pan and Collegiate Peaks wilderness areas. In fact, when you look down into Northstar Preserve it feels as if you are completely away from the town of Aspen.

At the base of Walsh's the run merges into Lud's Lane, which also collects skiers completing the other blacks, and runs toward Gentleman's Ridge, rated black diamond, as it continues along the ski-area boundary line. Here you get a chance to catch your breath. A short (16-yd/15-m) hike is required, slightly uphill, to where it intersects with Gentlemen's Ridge.

The traverse then skirts along the top of Gentlemen's Ridge, a tantalizing single-black-diamond-gladed bowl. Gentlemen's Ridge itself isn't supersteep until you go beyond the bottom of the Gentlemen's Ridge lift, after which it allows you to drop into any of the five black-diamond runs that take off on skier's left.

But you must stay focused: ignore these temptations until the next time and stay high on the eastern boundary line.

Continue straight in order to access the mystical terrain of Jackpot and Bingo Glades.

"In-boot pant skiers should not attempt this run"

Keep skier's right on the boundary and opt for Bingo Glades, which leads back down to the town. This area is secured by an access gate, closed if the terrain isn't safe, and complete with the standard warning sign that is more worth a read than most. After the usual blurb about unmarked obstacles, it provides some very useful advice: "In-boot pant skiers should not attempt this run." In other words, if you ski with your pants tucked into your ski boots, you're not going to be good enough to ski it.

So yank out your ski pant bottoms and enjoy this wonderful powder skiing through the aspen, spruce, and fir trees. From here you can begin to see out and glimpse the town of Aspen lying below you, imparting a very special feeling that you're skiing down to one of the world's great resorts.

One of the many great things about Bingo is that it's consistently steep the entire way down, although tree cover varies from quite spare to extremely tight. In the morning it is sheltered from the sun and there's cold, smoky snow in there, then the run gets full sun the entire afternoon. At its base Bingo Glades empties into Bingo Slot, which will take you past the bottom of the Bell Mountain chair and onto The Little Nell run. Mission accomplished, now let's do it again!

BELOW: Aspen, now one of the world's great ski resorts, used to be a small silver-mining town that was all but abandoned when the silver price plummeted in 1893. Above the town stands Aspen Mountain, with its access lifts starting yards from the main street.

Goat
Stowe, Vermont, USA
3,716ft (1,133m)

Although other resorts in eastern North America may have grown bigger over the years, none can compete with Stowe for its unique feel, an evermore valuable attribute in world skiing as fast lifts, snowmaking, and widened trails lead to ski areas increasingly feeling the same the world over.

Although the famous ski area in Vermont has recently invested hundreds of millions of dollars in bringing lifts, base facilities, hotels, and all other aspects of its operation up to the top end of 21st-century ski resorts, it remains famous for its movie-set standard, quintessentially New England village, along with its European feel that is thanks in part to the fact that many of the local lodge owners, most famously the Von Trapp family of *The Sound of Music* fame, are from Europe.

For skiers, though, it is famed for its classic New England terrain, particularly the Front Four double-black-diamond runs on which it has built its reputation as the real deal for good skiers.

Carving down the steep slopes of Mount Mansfield, the highest mountain in Vermont (4,392ft/1,339m), the first recorded ski descent of which was in 1914, these are assets that other resorts cannot create or buy. They help mark Stowe out as one of the special destinations of world skiing, putting it up near the top of every serious skier's bucket list.

The choice of four classics

What is a classic New England trail? Well, it's the antithesis of the wide, flat, modern runs created around the globe. Instead, it winds down through the trees, feeling narrow by modern standards, often with irregular fall lines and unusual pitches—in short, something that feels more natural, in tune with the lie of the original mountainside. The first trail to be cut specifically for skiing was created in 1933.

Stowe's Front Four built their reputation for being all that, but also for being (in contrast to most runs offered by other resorts in the region)

LEFT: Classic New England skiing means steep, narrow runs cut down through the trees with lots of deeply buried and snow-covered rocks, logs, and bumps in the ground to keep you on your toes.

RIGHT: While fresh snow can sometimes mean powder conditions, more often bumps form to provide a challenge and enjoyment of their own.

very steep and very long. Having a choice of four rather than just the one classic helps, too.

Those four nominees are Goat, Lift Line, National, and Starr (also known as International). But which of the four most deserves to be in our top 50?

The verdict of purists is that National and Lift Line are not what they once were. Piste widening and grooming (sacrilege!) have removed the challenge, with bumps less likely to be allowed to form (although perhaps those purists are looking back through rose-tinted goggles). That's not to say the challenge is not still there, with Lift Line infamous for an often icy sheet on its upper section thanks to wind exposure, but most would agree that the top spot is left to Starr or Goat.

Starr is still famed for its huge moguls which add to the impression, as you look in from the top, that the run is so steep you can't see the slope below—although rest assured, it does ease off after you make it past the first few. But Goat seems to be the trail that every good skier or boarder really gets. In Goat it all comes together—steepness, narrowness, tough fall line—almost every challenge

you can expect to come across on a ski run. There are unmarked obstacles, as clearly warned by signage at the top, accompanied by a neat picket fence rather than the usual rope to stop the inexperienced absent-mindedly setting off down. In short, you can expect everything bar an attack by a rampaging yeti—and even that might not come as a surprise.

The mogul empire

Goat is accessed by the FourRunner quad chairlift and is reputedly named because a visiting hiker in summer said that only a mountain goat would be able to climb it (if he or she mentioned skiing down it, that's not been recorded). It is one of the longest and steepest runs in New England, pitching at an average of 36 degrees with some sections hitting 40 degrees.

Along with the hazards of gradient, sometimes icy conditions and the creation of often humungous moguls, the warning sign at the top seeks to make those about to descend aware of the likelihood of exposed rocks, bits of trees, and other obstacles. Then there's the double fall line

LEFT: Although Stowe actually receives more than 26ft (8m) of snow on average each season, New England resorts do not have the deep-powder reputation of ski areas out west—so when it falls, it's extra special.

TOP RIGHT: A classic New England ski scene, with steep, narrow winding trails cutting down through the forest.

BOTTOM RIGHT: Stowe's steepest trails are a draw to every discipline in downhill snowsports. Alpine, snowboard, Telemark … it's all just as challenging, whatever you strap to your feet.

that tilts away to the left and the narrowness of the run to contend with. Cut as it is through the forest, it has not been widened like the other Front Four runs.

Goat has such a reputation that it is sometimes divided into two sections, Upper and Lower. Lower Goat, below the single-black-diamond Midway trail that dissects it two-thirds of the way down, is sometimes described as "twisting like a snake," providing ongoing hazards to negotiate, including several ledges and large rocks.

Heavy snow tends to make Goat marginally more skiable, and that's most likely in March when Vermont typically gets its greatest snowfall. Stowe can receive precipitation both from the Great Lakes and from the Atlantic, the latter usually bringing the greater volume, but Goat's hazards are so big that even deep snow doesn't cover them all.

Whatever the conditions, locals advise you keep left for the least challenging version of the descent, but whichever line you take be ready for a mental battle with yourself, as well as for the physical challenge that lies ahead.

Fact file Goat

IN SHORT: The toughest in the east

TOUGHNESS:
☠☠☠☠☠

FEAR FACTOR:
☠☠☠☠☠

VERTICAL:
3,716–1,715ft
(1,133–523m)
(2,001ft/610m vertical)

AVERAGE TIME:
15 minutes

LENGTH OF RUN:
0.62 miles (1km)

AVALANCHE KIT:
Nonessential

ACCESS:
FourRunner
quad chairlift

BEST TIME:
March is on average
Vermont's snowiest month

ALTITUDE RANGE: 787–
3,716ft (240–1,133m)

SKIABLE AREA:
39 miles (63km)

RUNS: 116

LIFTS: 13

WEB:
stowe.com

GETTING THERE:
Montreal
(136.4 miles/220km)

USA

MANSFIELD
1,339m ▲

START

GOAT

FINISH

Mount St. Elias
Canada/USA
18,004ft (5,489m)

AS ONE MEMBER OF THE TEAM BLUNTLY PUT IT: YOU CRASH, YOU'RE DEAD.

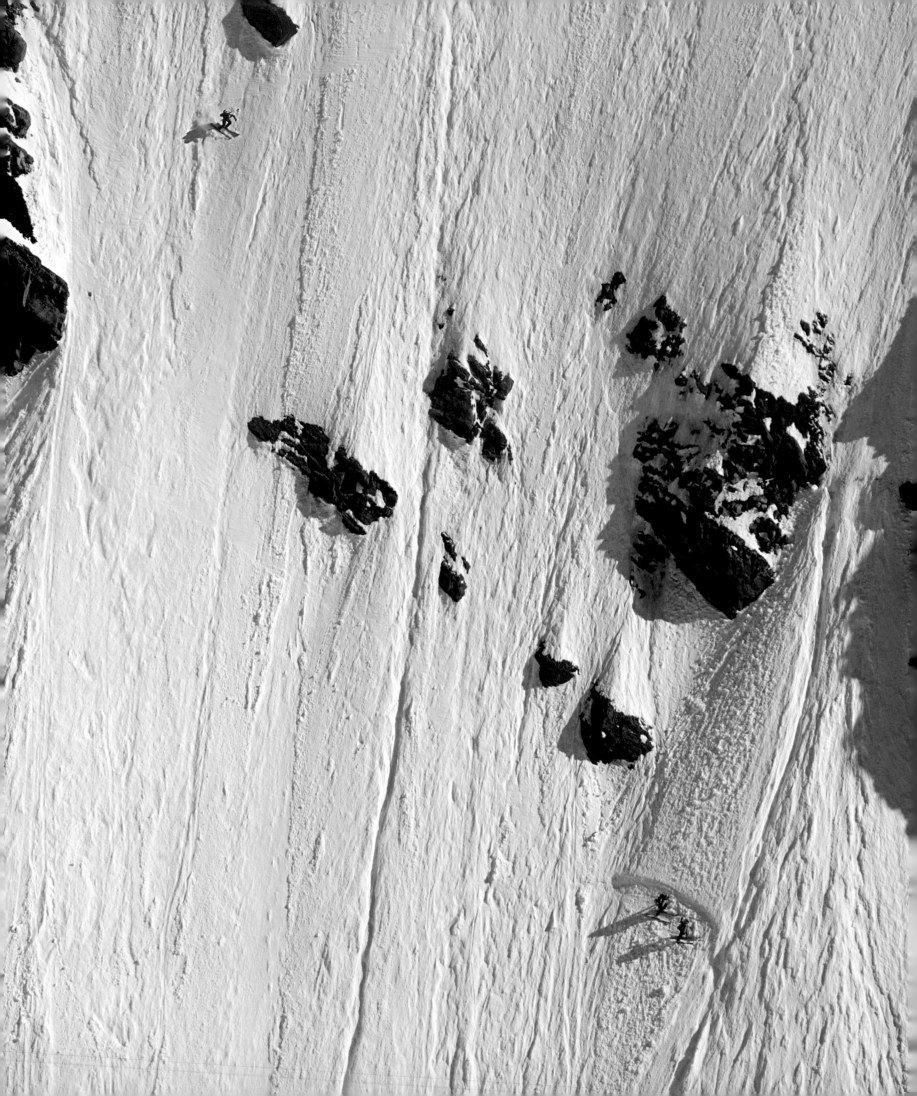

PREVIOUS PAGE: Nearing the top of the world's biggest skiable vertical, Mount St. Elias.

LEFT: Actually reaching the top of Mount St. Elias is one of the greatest challenges in ski mountaineering, then finding a clear day on which to ski down is another major obstacle, as waiting on the mountain is not recommended. The descent itself is also highly risky.

RIGHT: With no ski lift to take you to the summit of the world's highest vertical, these two thrill-seekers take on the grueling route, with the aid of ice axes.

O f the 50 runs in this book, 49 are skiable by most advanced skiers. It's true that, for most, you will need to be a very good skier to enjoy them—these are challenging slopes and not for novices, although some are doable even by intermediate skiers. But it seemed wrong not to include one run that is beyond most men or women, however experienced—not for the sake of including the nigh-on impossible, but in recognition of those extreme skiers who have, mostly in the last 20 years, tackled the world's highest and most dangerous descents, often losing their lives in the process.

The pioneers of 26,240ft (8,000m)

Among those first pioneers was the Frenchman Yves Morin, who became the first man to ski from above 26,240ft (8,000m). He descended from the summit of Annapurna in 1979, but died of exhaustion on the mountain the following day. His fellow Frenchman Marco Siffredi, who was the first to snowboard down Everest in 2001, disappeared while attempting to snowboard a different route from the world's highest peak the following year. The Swede Frederik Ericsson, meanwhile, died on his second attempt to ski K2 in 2010. All remain on those mountains.

But not everybody dies, and the Slovenian extreme skier Davo Karničar made it into the record books on November 11, 2006 when he skied Mount Vinson (16,062ft/4,897m) in Antarctica, having skied the seven highest peaks on each continent over the preceding seven years, starting with Mount Everest on October 7, 2000.

The longest vertical descent on the planet

The longest vertical descent is not, as many people might immediately think, on Mount Everest or indeed in the Himalayas at all. The highest mountains are there, of course, but they end at plateaus far above the tops of most mountains in the Alps. So on Everest, for example, the peak-to-base descent is 11,424ft/3,483m); not that much more than the world's biggest lift-served vertical at Chamonix, which is 9,207ft (2,807m).

In fact, the longest continually skiable vertical is in North America, where Mount St. Elias, lying on the Yukon/Alaska border and at 18,004ft (5,489m) the second-highest mountain in both Canada and the USA, is skiable (in the most liberal sense of the word) from top to bottom. However, attempting to do so and not losing your life is quite a challenge, and one that no one, so far, has completed in one go.

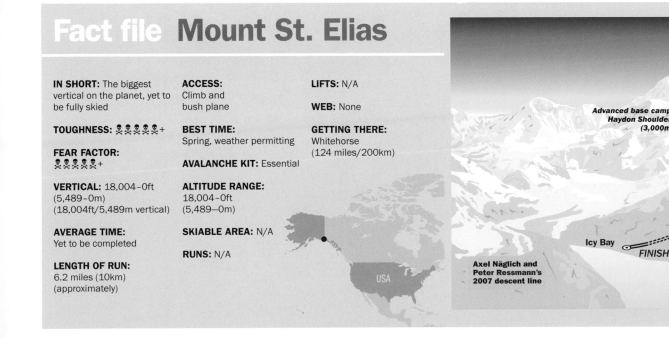

Fact file Mount St. Elias

IN SHORT: The biggest vertical on the planet, yet to be fully skied	**ACCESS:** Climb and bush plane	**LIFTS:** N/A
		WEB: None
TOUGHNESS: ☠☠☠☠☠+	**BEST TIME:** Spring, weather permitting	**GETTING THERE:** Whitehorse (124 miles/200km)
FEAR FACTOR: ☠☠☠☠☠+	**AVALANCHE KIT:** Essential	
VERTICAL: 18,004–0ft (5,489–0m) (18,004ft/5,489m vertical)	**ALTITUDE RANGE:** 18,004–0ft (5,489–0m)	
AVERAGE TIME: Yet to be completed	**SKIABLE AREA:** N/A	
	RUNS: N/A	
LENGTH OF RUN: 6.2 miles (10km) (approximately)		

MOUNT ST ELIAS ▲ 5,489m
START
Haydon Col (3,100m)
Advanced base camp Haydon Shoulder (3,000m)
Icy Bay
FINISH

Axel Näglich and Peter Ressmann's 2007 descent line

RIGHT: While offering the heaven of the world's biggest skiable vertical, Mount St. Elias is a mountain of hazards, making it hell to ski. These massive crevasses are just some of the many extreme challenges faced by those brave enough to tackle this uncharted ski territory.

The fearsome Mount St. Elias

The mountain is little known and even less frequently visited. The weather is generally terrible, with fog alternating with blizzards the norm and nighttime temperatures frequently at -40°F (-40°C). Actually climbing up it, let alone attempting to ski down it, is rarely attempted Still, this is the longest possible snow-covered vertical on the planet, going all the way down to sea level, in fact—some 18,001 vertical feet (5,488m)—so someone had to do it, and in 2000 somebody did. Well, most of it.

In May of that year, American ski mountaineers Lorne Glick, James Bracken, and Andy Ward made the summit and skied down 10,824 vertical feet (3,300m) over two days to the Bagely Icefield. The team skied down the Mira Face—rather ironically regarded as the "easy route." Lorne Glick would certainly disagree with that description—he later said that the gradient is such that a fall up there, " ... would be the end, no doubt." Among the hazards Glick noted is a rock band about a third of the way down the slope that is steeper than the slope and about 8ft (2.5m) wide. The trio began the descent partly roped together through a maze of huge cracks in the snow surface beneath the north face.

Two years later, ski mountaineers Aaron Martin and Reed Sanders also made the summit and attempted the ski down. After a few turns both began falling, and tragically their bodies are still somewhere on the mountain. As one member of the next team to attempt it bluntly put it, when describing the slope gradients of up to 65 degrees: "You crash, you're dead."

More widely publicized was the successful 2007 descent by the author of our foreword, the Austrian Axel Naglich, and his teammate Peter Ressman, for a movie by Gerald Salmina, entitled *Mount St. Elias*.

The duo of world-class adventurers skied most of it, but still didn't manage to descend the full vertical on skis, as the bottom 820ft (250m) close to sea level at Icy Bay was deemed unskiable. They had to do it in two separate sections, a month apart, the lower section (about 9,840ft/3,000m) in May and the upper section (about 6,560ft/2,000m) in the summer. It was a superhuman feat, however. Tragically, Ressman died a few years later in a very unfortunate climbing accident closer to home in Salzburg in 2010. All of which means that the full, top-to-bottom, 18,004-vertical-feet (5,489-m) ski descent of Mount St. Elias, the world's longest continuous vertical, is still up for grabs. Will you add it to your "must ski" list? You'd have to be at least as good as Axel Naglich and Peter Ressman, though. No, me neither.

Couloir Extreme
Whistler, Canada
7,495ft (2,285m)

W histler Blackcomb is one of the great success stories of North American skiing over the past three decades. It is the biggest ski area on the continent, with two glacier-capped mountains enabling it to offer summer skiing and boarding. It hosted the 2010 Winter Olympics and is home to 200 runs of all shapes and sizes. Which one to pick? I've opted for the obvious one: Couloir Extreme.

Although it's fair to say that Whistler Mountain has a slightly stronger reputation than Blackcomb for the extent of its steep terrain, the runs accessed from the 7th Heaven lift, the highest part of the entire ski region, include some of the very steepest, running down to Glacier Creek.

The most infamous of several very steep blacks here (including Big Bang and the Pakalolo Couloir), Couloir Extreme is arguably the toughest run in this vast ski area, in-bounds and marked on the piste map at least. And people do argue about that. Regardless, *Skiing* magazine lists it as one of the top ten steepest in-bounds runs in the world.

Before the run was officially added to the resort's terrain as a double-black-diamond route, it was originally named the Saudan Couloir by locals, in honor of Sylvain Saudan. The name was changed after the famous extreme skier reportedly complained about the unauthorized use of his surname.

As seen on TV

From 1987 the run, relatively newly opened up at the time, was the venue for the quickly infamous annual Saudan Couloir Extreme race, which started with the couloir but continued on below for 2,624 vertical feet (800m) to the bottom of the Jersey Cream chair. It became internationally famous and even warranted a 30-minute slot each spring on Canadian television.

LEFT: North America's largest ski area also has some of its steepest terrain, adding to its world-class reputation.

RIGHT: Whistler Blackcomb's average annual snowfall of nearly 39ft (12m), coupled with a wide selection of slopes, including several of the steepest you're likely to find at any ski area, are a winning combination for skiers and snowboarders in search of a great week in the mountains.

Accessed with a short ridge traverse from the top of the lift, this is one of the few runs where you can dodge under the rope, as it's there to add emphasis to the gradient that awaits below, rather than to say "closed" (unless it is). Numerous signs underlining the fact that this is steep and potentially dangerous terrain help to underline that message.

It's a run that is both superbly steep—pitching at up to 50 degrees with an average of 41 degrees—and wonderfully challenging: besides the gradient there are often gigantic moguls, concentrated particularly at the top to add to your alarm as you look in. These combine to make you feel that you're a million miles from anywhere, which is some achievement. Whistler Blackcomb is a big resort, attracting more than two million visitors each year, so finding a run where you feel away from it all is quite a trick.

Skiing is believing

As with many of the world's steepest runs, a big part of Couloir Extreme's challenges are the snow conditions and also, if you are technically able to ski it, the mental challenge of believing you can. The

top is the narrowest and steepest part of the run and often overhung with a cornice. If there's less snow, there may be more exposed rock to avoid. The best route in—presuming you're looking for the least testing —can vary depending on snow conditions and how usage by others has shaped the slope below. Typically, however, the way in is steeper to skier's left and easier to the right. After the initial steepest section the couloir widens out and becomes less vertiginous, mellowing out to around 40 degrees. But the run goes on and on, which some contend makes it better than some of the world's iconic couloirs that may be still steeper, but are short and sweet once you have gathered the bottle to jump in.

Such is the reputation of the run that different routes down it have been named, too—the Sylvain and Hawaii 5-0 lines are among the more difficult.

There is debate among Whistler Blackcomb fans as to whether Couloir Extreme or Spanky's is the more challenging and the more enjoyable. Spanky's is a large area with multiple routes down and therefore best tackled with a guide, especially the first few times.

LEFT: Couloir Extreme offers some heart-stopping turns on the way down, and if you catch the run early after a night of fresh snow, you'll be the first to make your mark.
BELOW: An Inukshuk—a stone cairn traditionally built by the indigenous peoples of the region—stands high on the slopes of Whistler Blackcomb, having been reinvented as a symbol of the 2010 Winter Olympics.

The gate-accessed run is reached with an uphill hike up Spanky's Ladder from the top of the same Glacier Express lift. For some of the steepest couloirs there, turn left once through the gate and follow the ridge until it ends and you're at the top of the Calvin & Hobbes Chute and the shorter Secret Chute, both reputedly steeper still than Couloir Extreme.

Limitless options

Then there are the catskiing and heliskiing possibilities. The options here are fairly limitless and, if you don't feel up to tackling the very steepest terrain on your arrival in town, this is also one of those resorts with a concentration of teachers and guides competing to give you the best possible tuition and raise your game so that, conditions permitting, you can tackle it by the end of the week.

These companies include Extremely Canadian, founded by a gentleman named Pete Smart who, despite his love of steep skiing, says it is worth going to the top just to take in the amazing 300-degree view of the Cascade Mountains. "It's the closest most people will get to standing on a spire," he says.

Fact file Couloir Extreme

IN SHORT: The closest most people will get to skiing down a spire

TOUGHNESS:
☠☠☠☠

FEAR FACTOR: ☠☠☠☠

VERTICAL:
7,492–6,101ft
(2,284–1,860m)
(1,391ft/424m vertical)

AVERAGE TIME: Ten minutes

LENGTH OF RUN:
0.74 miles (1.2km)

ACCESS:
7th Heaven chairlift

BEST TIME:
Usually March–May

AVALANCHE KIT:
Essential

ALTITUDE RANGE: 2,214–7,495ft (675–2,285m)

SKIABLE AREA:
8,172 acres (3,307ha)

RUNS: 200

LIFTS: 38

WEB:
whistlerblackcomb.com
whistler.com
extremelycanadian.com

GETTING THERE:
Vancouver
(84.3 miles/136km)

CANADA

BLACKCOMB
2,440m ▲

SPANKY'S LADDER

Horstman Hut

START

FINISH

COULOIR EXTREME

North Bowl
Revelstoke, Canada
7,675ft (2,340m)

" THE ABUNDANT POWDER STAYS FRESHER FOR LONGER THAN ON OTHER SLOPES ... IT WOULD BE A CRIME TO EVER GROOM IT. "

I n 2007, Revelstoke seemed to appear from nowhere to offer the biggest lift-served vertical in North America. The remarkable Revelation gondola, and the Stoke high-speed quad chair, opened up a superb 5,619 vertical feet (1,713m) between them. For an even longer descent, you can hike still higher.

To the global ski community's intelligentsia, who had been skiing on Mount Mackenzie for decades, Revelstoke wasn't such a surprise. Drawn by the area's reputation for seemingly endless slopes buried deep in light, fluffy, Pacific powder, they hiked and helicoptered into splendid isolation and some of the planet's most spectacular skiing. The area still lies at the heart of 494,200 acres (200,000ha) of heliski terrain.

In fact, Revelstoke's history as a snowsports destination dates back much further: skis were first brought here from Scandinavia in 1892 by a local miner. Not long after, the resort reached giddy heights, literally, as the home of Canada's main ski-jumping hill. This status continued for 60 years to the early 1970s, with five world records set there between 1916 and 1933; the first of these was claimed by Nels Nelsen, who jumped 184ft (56m) on the Revelstoke ski jump.

More recently, before the modern resort development, there was a rudimentary ski hill, with the majority of the now lift-accessible terrain belonging to a catskiing operation. So despite its status as "new," "unknown," and "North America's great skiing secret," the reputation for derring-do has been here in Revelstoke ("Revy" to its friends), for more than a century.

Steep powder

The snow has been falling in remarkable volumes here every winter for much longer than that. The 49ft (15m) of snow it averages puts Revelstoke in the world top five for quantity (it's light, fluffy, powdery stuff, too) and is another magnet for freeriders from around the world. Along with plenty of seriously steep terrain, the snowy abundance has helped it become one of less than half-a-dozen stops on the annual Freeride World Tour for the world's elite competitors in extreme snowsports. This is indeed something to witness, as competitors descend what they regard as one of the best venues on earth for their extreme skiing sport.

"[Revelstoke] is one of the most beautiful mountains we get to ski on the Tour and the snow in British Columbia is amazing," said Drew Tabke, winner of the Freeride World Tour here. So really, not a lot has changed since Revelstoke first gained its ski-jumping reputation 100 years ago.

Once you reach the top of the lift-served terrain, get off the Stoke chair and have North America's largest lift-served vertical at your feet. You'll have to hike anything from 15 to 45 minutes (depending on where you want to drop in) and up to 377 vertical feet (115m) to reach Sub Peak and the top of North Bowl (7,675ft/2,340m). Stoke chair is not difficult to find and, so efficient is the lift system serving the 59 long runs, that there's only one other chair needed on the upper mountain.

North Bowl offers some of the steepest terrain in North America and, thanks to its northerly orientation, the abundant powder stays fresher for longer than on other slopes; it would be a crime to ever groom it. The bowl stretches out below you in a natural amphitheater and you can pick your route down, opting for steep bowl skiing or taking in a cornice or cliff jump if you need a still bigger thrill.

The North Bowl is the *pièce de résistance* of Revelstoke. Contrary to its name, this is a steep and intimidating slope, often with the best snow conditions in the area.

RIGHT: Trees on upper runs in British Columbia can get so encrusted with snow that they are locally referred to as "snow ghosts."

LEFT: The blackest of black runs, Powder Assault is the steepest run on the already bloodcurdlingly steep North Bowl section of Revelstoke.

The longest vertical descent in North America

To make the full vertical of Revelstoke in one descent, you will need to keep skiing left. The routes have descriptive run names, including Parachute and Brake Check, and the main concern is to stop yourself from "going over the handlebars" on the steepest sections. Taking anything left of Sweet Spot inclusive will funnel you back to Downtowner, which wraps around the front of the mountain to connect with the lower section of the thigh-burner Pitch Black. The longest black on the mountain, right down to mid-mountain, Pitch Black is known for its smooth grooming and for being utter perfection with a few inches of fresh powder on top.

This full descent from the North Bowl makes for one awesome run of around 5,904 vertical feet (1,800m) in total. To make the most of North Bowl's full potential, though, you'll probably want to ski a few loops at the top, too—it extends for as far again into increasingly tight and challenging tree skiing through cedars if you don't take the turn out to meet Pitch Black. If you have the required cash, Revelstoke also offers both a catski and a heliskiing operation.

Locals also recommend forgetting the hike sometimes and instead taking some turns on the south side, where there's a choice of blacks and southwesterly winds often cause frontal snow deposits high up. There is lots of challenge and adventure to be had on that route, with loose glade and deep powder channels at the beginning, a combination of short, steep pitches and rollers with some moguls in the middle, and then a final flowing "off the beaten path" descent to the base—the only lower-mountain route that doesn't funnel to the mid-mountain lodge.

How long Revelstoke remains a secret remains to be seen; those who have spent millions on the resort obviously hope the crowds will arrive in ever greater numbers. However, the small, quirky town is a long way from anywhere—it's 297.6 miles (480km) from the intercontinental hub at Calgary and 124 miles (200km) from Kelowna, which is served by North American Airlines—and all that snow can make traveling to the resort a challenge in winter. The sense that you've escaped the rest of the world is certainly part of the appeal; it's still not unusual to find you're one of only a few hundred well-dispersed people on the mountain, if you visit outside vacation season—with that vast volume of powdery terrain seemingly yours alone.

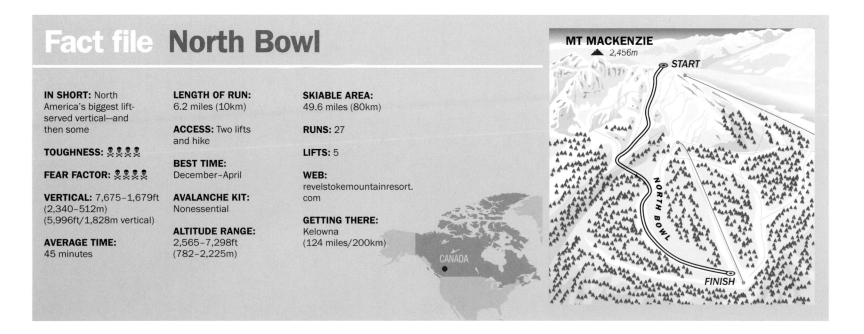

Fact file North Bowl

IN SHORT: North America's biggest lift-served vertical—and then some

TOUGHNESS: ☠☠☠☠

FEAR FACTOR: ☠☠☠☠

VERTICAL: 7,675–1,679ft (2,340–512m) (5,996ft/1,828m vertical)

AVERAGE TIME: 45 minutes

LENGTH OF RUN: 6.2 miles (10km)

ACCESS: Two lifts and hike

BEST TIME: December–April

AVALANCHE KIT: Nonessential

ALTITUDE RANGE: 2,565–7,298ft (782–2,225m)

SKIABLE AREA: 49.6 miles (80km)

RUNS: 27

LIFTS: 5

WEB: revelstokemountainresort.com

GETTING THERE: Kelowna (124 miles/200km)

MT MACKENZIE
▲ 2,456m
START

NORTH BOWL

FINISH

CANADA

I Gully, Whitehorn III
Lake Louise, Canada
8,649ft (2,637m)

LEFT: Lake Louise has a reputation for having not only some of the most spectacular steep skiing on the planet, but also some of the skiing world's greatest views.
RIGHT: Lake Louise not only offers its skiers and snowboarders steep chutes and extreme pitches, but you can also ski down a thigh-burning mogul run for a bit of variety.

Lake Louise is one of the few ski areas on the planet where you stand at the top of the ski run and think, "It doesn't get much better than this." It's not just that the scenery of the Canadian Rockies is definitely up there as among the best in North America, and indeed the world; nor the great powder snow record or even the fact that its protected National Park status means that from most of the ski area you can look out for miles and see little or no signs of human activity. It's a combination of all these things.

Having one of North America's biggest ski areas helps, too, and the tri-area Banff regional pass means that you can also ski Sunshine and Mount Norquay—each around half an hour away on fairly empty roads—on the one ticket. Although Lake Louise, with 4,201 acres (1,700ha) of terrain spread over four mountains and more than 100 marked runs, is a world-class ski area in its own right, of course.

Lake Louise has a reliable snowfall record that enables it to be one of the first on the continent to open in early November each year, and then to stay open for more than six months to early May. It's also the venue chosen by the International Ski Federation to host the first World Cup downhill races of the season in the northern hemisphere each fall.

Some of the world's greatest runs

So with World Cup race courses and a reputation for steep powder runs, there are plenty of candidates here for the world's greatest run, but I decided to plump for the only run in this book that has been christened by its avalanche control name: the I Gully, which runs from Whitehorn III into Whitehorn II.

Part of an area of Lake Louise known descriptively as The Back Bowls, Whitehorn II is around 0.62 miles (1km) across and contains eight steep gullies, each leading to some of the best powder stashes you're likely to find anywhere. It's well known to locals as the place to go to find powder, even if none has fallen from the sky recently.

Most of Lake Louise's wind comes from the southwest, and the gullies face more or less northeast. Wind hits the southwest slopes and picks up snow as it speeds up, then drops it on the other side (the gullies) as it slows down. This moving snow is called "fetch" (shorthand for, "fell in one place, transported by wind to another").

What each of the eight routes have in common, besides the powder, is the gradient. Located high above the treeline, they pitch at a seriously steep 45 degrees at the top, before easing out to marginally

Fact file I Gully

IN SHORT: One of the few lift-accessed runs in the world that's sometimes described as "better than heliskiing"

TOUGHNESS:
☠☠☠☠

FEAR FACTOR: ☠☠☠☠

VERTICAL: 8,446–7,446ft (2,575–2,270m) (1,000ft/305m vertical)

AVERAGE TIME: 15 minutes

LENGTH OF RUN: 656yd (600m)

ACCESS: Summit Platter lift

BEST TIME: Tends to get better as season progresses in normal year

AVALANCHE KIT: Essential

ALTITUDE RANGE: 5,399–8,649ft (1,646m–2,637m) (3,257ft/993m max vertical)

SKIABLE AREA: 4,201 acres (1,700ha)

RUNS: 139

LIFTS: 9

WEB:
skilouise.com
skibig3.com

GETTING THERE: Calgary (117.8 miles/ 190km)

CANADA

WHITEHORN
2,672m

START

WHITEHORN BOWL

MIDDLE-BACK BOWL

I GULLY, WHITEHORN

BOOMERANG BOWL

FINISH

more gentle terrain as the gullies meet in a glorious powder bowl—or a massive mogul field, if there's been no fresh snow for a while.

Most of the gullies have a small bowl feature at the top that leads into the narrow chutes between ridges. Where these ridges end are the areas known as the "fans," as this is where avalanching snow fans out after passing through the narrow gullies, and is also usually where most of the wind-blown snow accumulates.

Head left for powder

The gully names are the code names originally given by avalanche control, a simple matter of A Gully through to H Gully in Whitehorn II. At one point, these were given creative names corresponding to their letter such as Adrenaline, Chimney, Exit Only, Free Fall, and Gravity Pull, but they've now reverted to those initials. Whatever the name, the chutes tend to get more tricky the further down the alphabet you go.

Most difficult, however, is actually a ninth choice, the I Gully. This actually sits in the next area across—Whitehorn III—which is permanently closed due to avalanche danger, but I Gully merges at its base with H Gully, so is treated as one with the eight Whitehorn II gullies. Right on the edge of Whitehorn III, it is open when avalanche-safe. It has a narrow (just wider than a ski length), rocky entrance chute, and is steeper at the top than the others.

After a snowfall and once avalanche control work is done, locals will usually start with C Gully, as it is the one that is directly below the top of the Summit Platter lift, which accesses the summit. Then, on each concurrent lap, they'll move further to skier's left, and can often find fresh powder even days after a snowfall. In other words, to find the best powder, head left!

A dedicated avalanche team

Although people have been cross-country skiing in Lake Louise since the 1890s, with downhill introduced more than 90 years back and the first draglift built in 1954, Whitehorn II (and the I Gully of Whitehorn III) has only been officially open to skiers and included on the trail map for the past few years.

It's so steep that it used to be a permanent avalanche closure, and these days a dedicated team works hard to make it as avalanche-safe as possible each winter so that it can open. It was first opened for just a fortnight at the end of the season; then, as Lake Louise's ski patrol became ever more expert on the unique weather pattern and land structures in the area, Whitehorn II and Whitehorn III's I Gully have been able to open earlier and earlier—even, on good years, before Christmas.

RIGHT: The word "awesome" is commonly bandied about in North America, but the scenery of Lake Louise reminds us what the word should really be reserved for.

La Crête
Mont-Sainte-Anne, Canada
2,624ft (800m)

La Crête is not the steepest run, nor the most challenging that Mont-Sainte-Anne has to offer, or indeed that any of the several hundred ski centers in eastern Canada have in their quotas. But it does deliver what others do not: an incredible panorama of the mighty St. Lawrence river spread out below you as you descend its very satisfying 2.17-mile (3.5-km) length.

The Crête run is easy to reach from the ski area base, itself one of the easiest major resorts in the world to access, just 40 minutes from Quebec City international airport. Head straight for the eight-passenger gondola at the base and this will whisk you in less than five minutes to the top of the mountain. From here you traverse to skier's right, following the ridge and passing the top of nine or ten different black- and double-black-diamond descents, each also worthy of your attention at some point during your visit. This whole mountain face is known in French as the "Zone Expert" and contains the neighboring La S, La Super S, and Les Sept Chutes, for example, all served by their own quad chairlift. These will appeal even more to those living for steeps than La Crête; they just don't have the length, or the views.

So although our skis may attempt to drag us left into the fall line, we must hold firm, stick to the area boundary, and go past these runs, negotiate paragliders who'll be taking off if conditions are right, and go onto Le Chalet de La Crête, right at the start of the run, before beginning our descent.

La Crête is a relatively straightforward descent, graded black diamond at the top and great for high-speed cruising through its long, thigh-burning duration. Following the ski area boundary all the way back to the base, the greatest challenge can be if the temperatures drop to double digits below, as they can sometimes here, and the surface becomes slick and icy.

LEFT: Rising high above the St. Lawrence plain, there are huge sweeping views to take in as you whizz down Mont-Sainte-Anne's La Crête descent.

The legend of John the Hacker

The top of the run takes you through an area of the slopes known as the Black Forest. There's more to this sector than just the name, and you'd be right to think first of southern Germany's famous Black Forest region, as there is a dastardly German ghost haunting the slopes. This is something of a surprise when you consider that Quebec is historically best known for being fought over by the British and the French.

The story goes that "long, long ago," when Quebec was still under French rule, the French king sent a crack troop of soldiers across the Atlantic with the aim of ending the feuding in the New World. For some reason this crack troop included a German baron, one Johann von Hakken ("John the Hacker"), who had a bad reputation and, as

RIGHT: The mighty St. Lawrence River below dominates the vista from the slopes of Mont-Sainte-Anne.
BELOW: There are long midwinter nights at this latitude, but why stop skiing when you can floodlight the slopes?

tensions built up during the 13-week crossing, ended up killing the ship's captain and then escaping by canoe to the island of Sorciers in the St. Lawrence river below Mont-Sainte-Anne.

As time passed everyone thought von Hakken was either dead, eaten alive by wolves, or had escaped south to New England, but in fact he had changed his name to the more friendly French Jean de la Hache ("John of the Axe") and was still very much alive, living on Sorciers.

The curse of the Black Forest

However, by the time the ski season rolled around, Jean was fed up of the island and wanted off. He set out across the ice toward Mont-Sainte-Anne, planning to hide up in the mountains just where the Black Forest is now. He miscalculated the thickness of the ice, however, and the effect upon it of the tide. Halfway across, the ice broke and Jean fell into the river.

Even then, all was not lost. A sorcerer appeared and offered the drowning man the chance to escape to the mountains he was aiming for; he just had to give the sorcerer his eternal soul. The deal was done and ever since, Johann von Hakken has been roaming the woods of the Black Forest, raging among the trees, working endlessly on a passageway through the forest that could set him free of Mont-Saint-Anne, and return him to the island to get his old body back and head home to the Old World (so he must have been grateful when the ski area opened and the trails were cut straight down).

Sadly for Johann though, he is never able to reach the coast of the river—each time he gets to the edge of the Black Forest, he is magically thrown back to its highest peak, even without the use of the gondola.

People from every generation have reported feeling his presence as they ski down, so remember to look out for him and give him a wave if you see him as you whizz past. You'll also notice that some of the runs are named in his memory—Triumph, Munster, and Schnell.

There is one bit of the legend to be wary of if you're skiing down around lunchtime. Hakken is reported to have discovered a way to escape the sorcerer's curse. He needs to ski or board down the mountain on the shoulders of someone who, at noon precisely and when the wind is blowing from the north, looks from the top of the mountain directly to the west. You have been warned!

Fact file La Crête

IN SHORT: For breathtaking views of the mighty St. Lawrence, with a ghost included, it doesn't get better than this

TOUGHNESS: ☠☠

FEAR FACTOR: ☠☠

VERTICAL: 2,624–574ft (800–175m) (2,050ft/625m vertical)

AVERAGE TIME: Ten minutes

LENGTH OF RUN: 2.17 miles (3.5km)

ACCESS: Gondola lift and quad chairlift

BEST TIME: All season

AVALANCHE KIT: Nonessential

ALTITUDE RANGE: 574–2,624ft (175–800m)

SKIABLE AREA: 526 acres (213ha) skiable

RUNS: 67

LIFTS: 10

WEB: Mont-Sainte-anne.com

GETTING THERE: Quebec (34.7 miles/56km)

CANADA

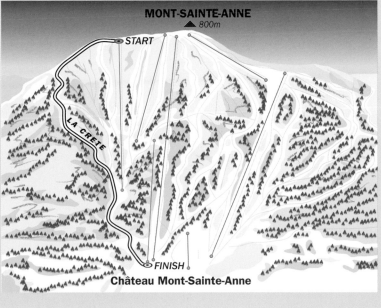

MONT-SAINTE-ANNE
▲ 800m

START

LA CRÊTE

FINISH
Château Mont-Sainte-Anne

Northern Europe

The area around Lyngen Lodge in Norway offers some of the most remarkle skiing adventures you could ever hope for in Scandinavia.

Revelation
Kangaamiut, Greenland
6,560ft (2,000m)

With up to 20 hours of daylight on offer and as a result of its geographical isolation, skiing in Greenland, one of the most remote locations on Earth, is a truly magical experience.

With much of the country covered in ice and snow all year round, and the mountains on its east coast rising to the 12,116-ft- (3,694-m-) high Gunnbjørn Fjeld, emerging through the glacial ice and the highest mountain north of the Arctic Circle, Greenland should be a good ski destination.

And indeed it is. It is just that, given its small population and global isolation, not enough people want to go there to make a commercial ski area viable, although half-a-dozen draglifts are dotted around the coast close to the larger communities. But if you're looking for a unique experience, that seclusion from the rest of the world is a good thing.

What you need to access the vast powder fields that tumble down for up to 6,560 vertical feet (2,000m) to the coast is either the patience and skill to climb up or, better still, a helicopter.

18-hour days

For more than a decade now, Greenland Heliskiing have been providing just that opportunity, one of just a handful of very small expert local operators that can offer heliskiing here. Based on the west coast (where attracting polar bear attention is not a problem) rather than the east, in a village in the Eternity Fjord on the small island of Kangaamiut, 37.2 miles (60km) north of the larger (but still pretty tiny) village of Maniitsoq and just south of the Arctic Circle, the company runs tours in mid-spring each year. This is when the temperatures are warmer, the snow pack more secure and daylight lasts 18–20 hours, giving plenty of scope for longer adventures.

The company chose Kangaamiut as they found a great mix of terrain there, from steep couloirs to long, gentle glaciers ideal for high-speed cruising and everything in between. The peaks are rugged and the terrain vast, with 927 square miles (2,400 square km) of pristine peaks above 6,560ft (2,000m) in the local area alone.

More than ten years after arriving, groups are still finding new routes for first descents every season. Indeed, with the slowly moving glaciers and the opportunity to constantly try new routes, naming a particular run is not as clear-cut here as for a conventional ski resort.

In fact there are hundreds of different glacial runs dropping into three different fjords directly behind the Island, which is capped by the 6,560-ft- (2,000-m-) high Adam Peak. Many of the runs end down at sea level, most with views out to sea where vast icebergs may be floating by and you may even see the odd whale or two break the surface. Typically, north facing slopes offer powder-snow conditions even in May, when temperatures are still normally just below freezing at sea level and cooler as you ascend. South-facing slopes have typical spring "corn snow."

Skiing above the precipice

The descent named Revelation is a particular favorite. From a peak at 5,445ft (1,660m), the run starts out on really mellow terrain—hence the peak's name, "Flat Top." Floating down the initially gentle slope warming up with long giant-slalom turns, little do you realize that you are skiing above a 1,640-ft (500-m) cliff leading directly to the Eternity Fjord below.

BELOW: The crevasses on this run come thick and fast as you round the mountain and are often almost invisible from above, so an experienced local guide is essential to navigate these more treacherous parts.

" YOU NEED TO BE VERY FIT, ABLE TO
HANDLE ALL TYPES OF CONDITIONS, AND
HAVE FULL BACKCOUNTRY SKIING EXPERIENCE.
THIS IS A SERIOUS EXPEDITION. "

There is one tiny keyhole passage off this plateau, a steepish couloir that feeds into the wide-open slopes below. This new view of the fjord below your skis creates fresh emotions. Part-way down these powdery slopes, traverse right to gain another flank of the mountain, previously hidden from view. After skiing this steep slope for another 1,640ft (500m), you are spat out onto the final 1.24 miles (2km) of wide-open glacier, leading to the waiting chopper at the water's edge.

Now we know the reason for the name "Revelation": it's because with each new twist and turn, a new hidden passage reveals itself on your way to the sea. It's a mountain guide's dream line.

And you will need a mountain guide in order to explore the region fully and take advantage of a helicopter if it's pure downhill skiing you came here for. Greenland Heliskiing is one of a few companies that operate in the region, but there are also international operators such as Arctic Heliskiing that offer Greenland heliskiing deals. Depending on your level of skiing experience, these operators all offer sound advice for the best choice of area and run, and also supply experienced guides as part of their deal.

The full backcountry experience

The skiing on Revelation is not for the inexperienced or the unfit—you need to be the exact opposite, in fact: very fit, able to handle all types of conditions, and have full backcountry skiing experience. This is a serious expedition. The cost of organizing the trip means that you need to be quite well-heeled, too. Fat skis cope best with the deep powder and all participants need to be equipped with avalanche transceiver, probe, and shovel. The company provides everyone with avalanche backpacks containing airbags. As the terrain is glaciated, an Alpine harness has to be worn while you ski, so that you can be fished out more easily if you fall into a crevasse.

The full Greenland Heliskiing experience is not just about heliskiing, but about living with the local population and enjoying traditional meals at the end of the day. These use ingredients sourced in the area, with halibut, musk ox, and reindeer all on the menu. And icebergs and whales may not be all you'll see: during the short nights, the northern lights may put in an appearance. Truly a once-in-a-lifetime, and indeed potentially life-changing experience.

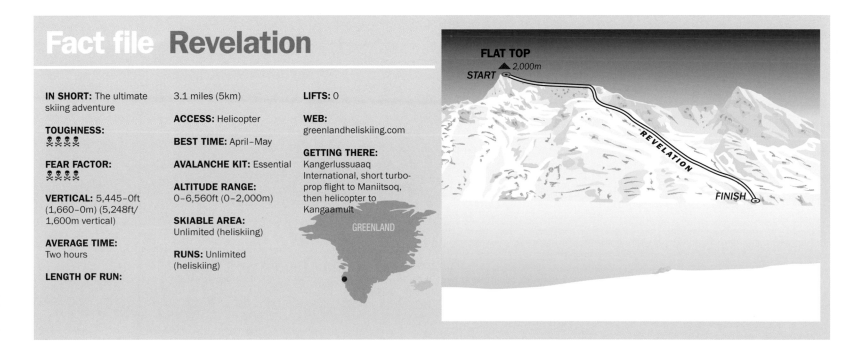

Fact file Revelation

IN SHORT: The ultimate skiing adventure

TOUGHNESS:
☠☠☠☠

FEAR FACTOR:
☠☠☠☠

VERTICAL: 5,445–0ft (1,660–0m) (5,248ft/ 1,600m vertical)

AVERAGE TIME:
Two hours

LENGTH OF RUN:
3.1 miles (5km)

ACCESS: Helicopter

BEST TIME: April–May

AVALANCHE KIT: Essential

ALTITUDE RANGE:
0–6,560ft (0–2,000m)

SKIABLE AREA:
Unlimited (heliskiing)

RUNS: Unlimited (heliskiing)

LIFTS: 0

WEB:
greenlandheliskiing.com

GETTING THERE:
Kangerlussuaaq International, short turbo-prop flight to Maniitsoq, then helicopter to Kangaamuit

GREENLAND

FLAT TOP
▲ 2,000m
START

REVELATION

FINISH

Lyngen Peninsula
Karlsøy, Norway
6,016ft (1,834m)

The remarkable Lyngen Peninsula offers ski
and snowboarding experiences like no other,
with abundant virgin powder slopes accessed
by boat, not ski lift.

There are ski vacations and then there are life-changing experiences—and skiing from a base at Lyngen Lodge within the Arctic Circle of northern Norway falls into the latter category for many of the people lucky enough to ski there. No ski lifts, no other people, in fact, and you take a boat across the Lyngen Fjord to reach the ski slopes. It's a very different experience.

It gets more remarkable still when you factor in that a visit in winter can mean skiing the virgin powder beneath the northern lights, or if you arrive in late spring, when 24 hour daylight is the norm, you can do it all under the midnight sun. And it all takes place against the backdrop of some of the most dramatic and spectacular scenery on Earth, with white mountains towering out of the sea.

The skiing day at Lyngen typically involves a 15–45-minute boat trip aboard the 36-ft- (11m-) long Spirit of Lyngen from the Lodge to the base of the selected ski mountain. The boat has been specially designed to enable skiers to be deployed directly from the bow onto beaches to begin their three-to-four hours of skinning up 3,280–4,264 vertical feet (1,000–1,300m) for their descent. To be able to do this, of course, the fitter you are the better. You also need to be at least a strong off-piste skier, although the Lodge offers beginner-level ski touring (as well as all levels above) and on-site rental of the best equipment for the conditions and you are accompanied by fully qualified mountain guides. Because you're closer to sea level than in the Alps, of course, you'll also find you have around 20 percent more energy to do it all.

Fresh tracks

Choosing *the* run for the Lyngen Alps is a difficult choice, as you will almost invariably be making fresh tracks and there are more than 60 summits over 3,280ft (1,000m) accessible from the Lyngen Fjord's

shores. Most of the peaks reach a maximum of 3,936ft (1,200m); at 6,016ft (1,834m) Jiehkkevárri is the highest, and the highest glaciers of the main Lyngen Peninsula reach over 4,592ft (1,400m). So there are many more than 50 great runs in the Lyngen Alps alone. But for the sake of choosing one, perhaps we'll go with the Lodge's "home mountain" of Storhaugen, the 3,746-ft (1,142-m) peak of which is reached directly with a three-hour climb via the west face on skis without needing the boat trip. Classic ski descents on the west and north sides, which hold the snow well through to late spring, are possible. From the top, where a large summit-ridge cornice forms, there's an average (and fairly consistent) slope angle of 30 degrees on the long, open slopes, with some tree skiing on lower sections. Just to add to the pleasure, there are phenomenal views across to the island of Uløya and the Lyngen Alps as you descend.

Another contender is the island of Kågen, the west coast of which is accessed by boat from the Lodge. It is regarded by ski-touring purists as perhaps the world's best skiing island, with the run down the northeast glacier from the summit of Storekågtinden at 4,028ft (1,228m) particularly recommended. It's usually completed in powder snow due to the sheltered and northerly aspect.

Make a first descent

If you want to really push the boat out, the area is so underexposed to ski tourism that there are still first descents to be made. A recent one saw two Brits ski the 2,624-ft- (800-m-) long Milbourne Couloir on the east face of Stor Reindalstinden, which rises 4,405ft (1,343m) from the ocean and offers challenges including cliff bands, couloir systems, and pitches of up to 55 degrees.

When to visit is another tough choice. The season begins in February when it can be very cold with limited daylight hours, although the polar light at this time of year has its own magic. The snow in February is especially crisp and the Gulf Stream stops it getting as cold as is usually the case in midwinter, 310 miles (500km) north of the Arctic Circle. By mid-February there are already seven hours of daylight and you have the best chance of seeing the northern lights. From mid-April you can enjoy long days and spring snow on the north-facing slopes, the only downside being that the snowline may move above sea level, so there can be a hike back at the end of your run. Arrive from May and you can head out skiing at 10 p.m., skin up until 1 a.m., and ski down under the midnight sun.

Just to ensure complete perfection, Lyngen Lodge itself offers luxurious accommodation with gourmet cuisine; altogether, a skiing experience you do not want to miss out on.

TOP LEFT: The remote location of Lyngen Lodge, and the little light pollution this affords, make it one of the top ski destinations for seeing the aurora borealis.
LEFT: One of the many superb steep slopes down to the sea on the Lyngen Peninsula.
RIGHT: This large summit-ridge cornice is a good choice during challenging avalanche conditions, providing you have the experience to choose an appropriate route.

Fact file Lyngen Peninsula

IN SHORT: Ski to the sea, stay in luxury on skis

TOUGHNESS: ☠☠☠ to ☠☠☠☠☠

FEAR FACTOR: ☠ to ☠☠☠☠☠

VERTICAL: 4,028–0ft (1,228–0m)

AVERAGE TIME: 40 mins

LENGTH OF RUN: 2.48 miles (4km)

ACCESS: Boat and ascent

BEST TIME: February–May

AVALANCHE KIT: Essential

ALTITUDE RANGE: 0–6,016ft (0–1,834m)

SKIABLE AREA: Unlimited, ski touring

RUNS: Unlimited, ski touring

LIFTS: 0

WEB: lyngenlodge.com

GETTING THERE: Tromsø (115.3 miles/186km)

NORWAY

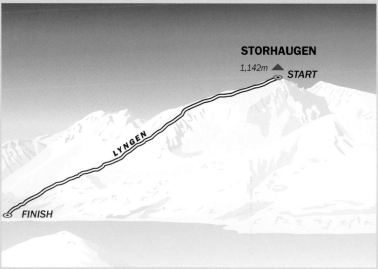

STORHAUGEN
1,142m ▲ START

LYNGEN

FINISH

Lundsrappet
Åre, Sweden
4,179ft (1,274m)

BELOW: It can get a bit cold in these northern latitudes, but on the upside, the snow stays crisp and fresh.

RIGHT: The most visited ski area in Scandinavia has something for every type and ability of skier and snowboarder—the famous Hummelbranten mogul run for bumps, heliskiing, and famed off-piste options for powder and the near-perfect Lundsrappet for speed.

Scandinavians have more than 600 ski areas to choose from, albeit most of them are rather small areas, but around a quarter of all skiers head to just one resort, the biggest, as they have been doing since 1910: Åre in Sweden.

Åre, pronounced "oar-er" and short for Årefjällen, consists of five separate villages below a large ski area spreading for many miles along the mountainside above the huge, frozen Lake Åresjön, which stretches all the way to the Norwegian border in the west. The northerly latitude means a six-month ski season is the norm, with low temperatures keeping the snow in great shape.

The resort is an historic one, with tourism beginning in the 1880s when the railroad reached the town. Even today, it's popular to take the overnight train up from Stockholm and either dance all night in the disco car or relax in the sleeper. Daytime services are also good, and a high-speed version now makes the 327-mile (600-km) trip in five-and-a-half hours. The funicular railroad, opened in 1909, still accesses the slopes. Architecturally, the resort is a mix of old wooden buildings and modern additions. The resort center around the railroad station square is especially attractive and buzzing at *après-ski* time.

A high-speed descent

In terms of great runs, there is a feast of riches here. The resort not only has heliskiing and famed off-piste options, in particular the 4.9-mile (8-km) descent to the neighboring village of Huså, but among the

100-plus pistes to choose from there's the famous Hummelbranten mogul run. Åre is also a frequent host of World Cup racing and has staged the Alpine Skiing World Championships twice, in 1954 and 2007, and hopes to do so for a third time. Skiers reach 74.4 miles (120 km) per hour and encounter some of the biggest jumps on the World Cup circuit here. So powder, bumps, or speed? I've opted for the last.

Why? The Lundsrappet is a near-perfect run for those who love high-speed, full-on, classic descents. It follows the same line as Åre's World Cup Stortloppet run, which is located next to it on skier's left, but is normally closed to mere mortals and only available on race days and for official race training.

It is a relatively simple slope, wide, and tree lined, with much of it just going straight down the mountainside above the lake, following the fall line, with little to divert you from the pure pleasure of skiing or boarding fast. After a short run across to its start from the top of the high-speed eight-seater VM8 detachable chairlift that runs its full length, you can look down from top to bottom, with the lake stretched out beyond, and just go. The upper section is the steeper, very black, but it mellows out to a slightly more gentle pitch, so if you go fast from the top you can control your speed, rather than have the slope fall away from you. It's the most beautifully simple run in this book.

Make it 2,624ft (800m) of vertical

But you can complicate things if you like, and add to the 1,476-ft (450-m) vertical descent by skiing another red/black from the top of the Åretopp Plata to gain the full near-2,624ft (800m) of vertical. Adding the Roda Rappet or the upper part of the Stortloppet runs to your route involves a gondola ride across the barren upper mountain, but you are rewarded with still more impressive views from the top and a sweeping red-grade piste across the open mountainside above the treeline before you take a right turn onto the top of Lundsrappet.

But for Lundsrappet alone, the fast lift, floodlighting for night skiing, and an option to take a special, early-morning tour with a ski school from 7.30 a.m., mean that this run can be skied not only for up to six months of the year but also for 12 hours or more per day in peak season when the lifts run until 8 p.m. With that fast lift easily gobbling up any attempt at a queue building, you can make more laps of this perfect piste than almost any other.

Fact file Lundsrappet

IN SHORT: Seat-of-your-pants, high-speed skiing

TOUGHNESS: ☠☠☠

FEAR FACTOR: ☠☠☠

VERTICAL: 2,768–1,279ft (844–390m) (1,489ft/454m vertical)

AVERAGE TIME: Five minutes

LENGTH OF RUN: 0.74 miles (1.2km)

ACCESS: VM8 high-speed, eight-seat chairlift

BEST TIME: November–May

AVALANCHE KIT: Nonessential

ALTITUDE RANGE: 1,279–4,179ft (390–1,274m)

SKIABLE AREA: 62 miles (100km)

RUNS: 102

LIFTS: 47

WEB: skistar.com/are

GETTING THERE: Õstersund (62 miles/100km), Stockholm by train (372 miles/600km/5.5 hours)

SWEDEN

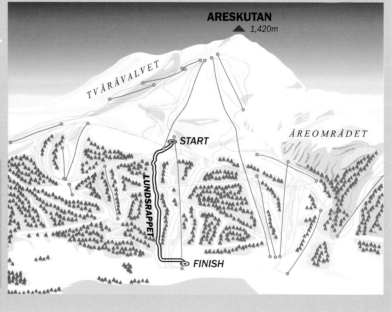

ARESKUTAN
▲ 1,420m

TVÄRÄVALVET

ÅREOMRÅDET

START

LUNDSRAPPET

FINISH

Coire Dubh
The Back Corries, Scotland
4,005ft (1,221m)

It is not uncommon for people who have skied at one of Scotland's five centers to report on some of the natural challenges that can be faced if the weather is not kind. The wooden tips of picket snow fences erected to try to stop snow from being blown off the mountain, but sticking up through the snow along with rocks and heather, can be a challenge even on the country's gentlest runs, as can the windchill, which can be extreme. Britain's strongest ever gust of wind, at 172.4 miles (278km) per hour, was recorded at Cairngorm summit above Aviemore on March 20, 1986.

If I'm painting a picture of Scottish conditions as typically terrible, I do the centers a disservice, as the obverse side of the coin includes deep powder days under blue skies with not a breath of wind, giving skiers or boarders the feeling that they're the luckiest people alive to be on the slopes that day.

Ski here and you can ski anywhere

Along with those occasionally extreme weather conditions, Scotland does offer ski slopes, on- and off-piste, that provide as much challenge as the toughest in the Alps or the Rockies. It is true what they say: "If you can ski in Scotland, you can ski anywhere."

Each center has one or more steep slopes and opinion is divided on which is the toughest. Cairngorm has the West Wall in Coire na Ciste Gully, Glenshee the mogulled Tiger, and Glencoe's well-titled Flypaper has gained the admiration of many serious skiers as one of the world's toughest marked runs. Its gradient, reputedly the steepest slope in Scotland, is such that it cannot be groomed, yet moguls cannot form to make descending easier as they do on many other famous blacks. There's a particularly steep, if short, line if you traverse out above the entrance to the Glas Maol black and then head straight down.

Beyond these ski area steeps, there are innumerable serious descents for ski tourers prepared to hike up across the Highlands.

RIGHT: The name and the signs say it all if you're wise enough to read and listen—underestimate Scottish terrain at your peril!

CHANCER

This is an off piste area
with challenging terrain.

Entry points are steep and
snow conditons can vary

Check with ski patrol for
up to date conditions.

Such are the challenges on offer, it's a shame that more coverage is not given to Scotland's runs in the London-centric ski travel media.

Having to choose one area of the many, I have opted for the Back Corries in the Nevis Range, partly for the challenge and the powder potential, but also for the spectacular views out over Scotland's west coast, to the edge of the Atlantic and the Isles, that you get as you ascend the slopes at Nevis. It is one of the greatest views in world skiing.

Take a look at some images of the top of the Back Corries, which are accessed by the rustic Braveheart chair, and you could be forgiven for thinking, at first glance, that you are looking down into Corbet's Couloir at Jackson Hole. The key difference to Jackson's infamous drop-in, however, is that the Corries are not limited to a narrow cleft in the rock but are accessed from a long ridge, and to some extent the size of the drop depends on how big a cornice has formed along the top.

Seriously off-piste

But before you leap, you need to look and know where you are. The legal status of the Back Corries is a tad complex, as while they can all be considered seriously "off-piste," they include the Coire Dubh, located within the ski-area boundary—thus, ensuring it is safe to ski is the responsibility of the management. However, the Back Corries also include the Summit Corrie and Coire an Lochan, reached by a short walk across the summit plateau. These are officially outwith the ski area and skied entirely at your own risk.

Coire Dubh was officially redesignated an "off-piste bowl" from the start of winter 2011–12. The entrances from Lemming Ridge are the steepest and most often corniced, with very variable snow conditions and the constant possibility of avalanche, although the in-bounds area is closed when the danger is thought to be above minimal risk. Before you start, you need to fully scope the drop and your landing area and work out your exit strategy if it doesn't go as you imagine.

LEFT: In a good year, the snow on Scottish slopes can equal the deepest in the world; add in a steep pitch and you have very challenging terrain.

ABOVE: There is only one place on Earth where you can hit the slopes in the morning with the most stunning views over the lochs, have some haggis for lunch, and enjoy a special kind of *après ski* at a local céilidh dance in the evening.

If you wish to avoid the cornice, there are usually options from the Switch run, where no vertical descent to the top of the slope is required —just the bottle to leap from the horizontal onto the top of the slope, the steepest section where those with clinometers have found pitches of between 45 and 50 degrees for the first 131ft (40m) or so, before easing slightly to an average 35-degree pitch. If that's soft powder, it can be beautiful; if it's hard packed and icy, it's a technical challenge.

When Braveheart is open you can ski the full vertical of Coire Dubh/Coire an Lochan and the Summit Coire, and be lifted back to the traverse out. When the chair is not open, you can still ski the upper slopes of Coire Dubh and exit without a walk.

Pick your line carefully

Whichever route you opt for, however, each of the corries should be treated as serious backcountry. You should be able to make good judgment on how to pick your line and ski this kind of terrain—and most importantly know the signs of when not to. You should also carry a transceiver, probe, and shovel and know how to use them if the worst should happen. The Nevis Range actually run dedicated "Back Corrie workshops" several times each season, where you can learn the best ways to enjoy the corries with maximum personal safety.

You should check conditions before venturing off-piste or into the backcountry, including checking the Nevis Range snow report and the Sportscotland Avalanche Information Service daily reports, with first-hand advice willingly provided by members of ski patrol, too.

Ski patrol do work in the Coire Dubh but, as with marked itinerary runs in the Alps, the cover is less comprehensive than on the marked, groomed runs on the front side of the mountain. Cover depends on the status of the corries on any one day, which is described in the daily snow report and fairly self-explanatory — "open" means full cover; "closed" means dangerous conditions and no cover and you lose your ski ticket if you try to ski them anyway; and "limited patrol" means just that, although the corries are open and ski patrol will assist anyone in difficulty.

Fact file Coire Dubh

IN SHORT:
Sensational snow and spectacular views from Scotland

TOUGHNESS:
☠☠☠☠

FEAR FACTOR: ☠☠☠☠

VERTICAL: 3,838–2,378ft (1,170–725m) (1,460ft/445m vertical)

AVERAGE TIME: 5 mins

LENGTH OF RUN:
0.74 miles (1.2km)

ACCESS: Gondola, then front-face lifts to Summit tow

BEST TIME: Usually January–April

AVALANCHE KIT:
Essential

ALTITUDE RANGE: 2,099–4,005ft (640–1,221m)

SKIABLE AREA:
9.3 miles (15km)

RUNS: 35

LIFTS: 12

WEB: nevisrange.co.uk winterhighland.info

GETTING THERE:
Inverness (62 miles/100km), Glasgow (111 miles/179km), Fort William rail station (6.8 miles/11km)

SCOTLAND

BEN NEVIS/BIEN NIBHEIS
▲ 1,344m

AONACH MOR

START

BACK CORRIES

FINISH
Braveheart

Western Europe

Luis Arias
Baqueira Beret, Spain
8,233ft (2,510m)

Baqueira Beret is home to one of the most magnificent ski areas in Spain—some will say the entire world. The Pyrenees have a rich mixture of terrain from beginner-friendly to steeps that even mountain goats have trouble clinging onto.

t's fair to say that among the uninformed, Spain is better known for its sunshine than its skiing. But nonetheless there are more than 30 ski areas dotted around the country, including Europe's most southerly in the Sierra Nevada, and the famous Baqueira Beret in the Pyrenees which has the royal seal of approval; the Spanish royal family come here each winter, just as the British one heads to Klosters.

As a result the most sought-after sector of the resort is known as La Pleta del Rey, which means "the king's hamlet." Originally it was King Juan Carlos who was a frequent visitor to the royal chalet here, but these days you are more likely to find you are sharing a chairlift with Crown Prince Felipe, next in line to the Spanish throne, or his sisters Princesses Elena and Cristina.

Baqueira was established in 1964 by a former Spanish ski champion, Luis Arias, who chose the resort's location to best take advantage of its exposure to heavy, snow-bearing clouds coming off the Atlantic every winter season. Then he built his base village with an eye to tasteful design in local wood and stone at a time when most European resorts were opting for a more Bauhaus-inspired stark and rectangular concrete.

Modern slopes and longer hours

The resort's southerly latitude means that skiing here can last longer each day than in the Alps—by springtime, there's up to an hour's difference in the daylight Baqueira receives. It's usually warmer, too, but snow cover is not normally a problem as the slopes face north or northwesterly and the ski runs are up to 8,233ft (2,510m) above sea level. Moreover, the extensive slope network coupled with an ultra-modern, comfortable, high-speed lift network makes getting around fast and easy.

For expert skiers, Baqueira Beret's off-piste terrain away from the groomed runs has a global fan base, with long, powdery descents through the wild and beautiful Arán valley where it is located. Here there are imaginatively and possibly accurately named couloirs including Ecornacrabes, which translates as "where goats fall."

Unlike over the border in France (where heliskiing is banned), the well-heeled can also rent a helicopter to lift them to fresh powder fields for their exclusive use.

But even without a helicopter you can access wonderful terrain on or off the piste. The mile-long Luis Arias black, named in honor of the great man, is extremely steep and remarkably straight, visible for most of its route from

LEFT: Baqueira Beret's slopes extend for 74.4 miles (120km) across rolling terrain above and below the treeline. Besides the 1.48-mile (2.4-km) Luis Arias racing piste, the resort is famous for its excellent and challenging freeride terrain.

RIGHT: Warm, moist air moving east from the Atlantic and then across the Spanish plain often deposits huge snowfalls on the Pyrenees, as the clouds are forced to rise and shed their snow as they hit the mountains. Thus, Europe's more southerly ski areas often receive much more snow than those in drier locations close to the Arctic Circle up in the far north of the continent.

the Jorge Jordana chairlift that runs directly back up above it for most of its length, making it easy to make laps, and to watch others descend.

The piste starts off wide and misleadingly gentle from the Cap de Baqueira, but funnels to a narrower width and the first of the steep "wall" sections before switching to skier's left and then swinging back right and under the chair halfway down. This is where the piste reaches its most challenging and steepest section.

Here it makes a steep, 90-degree turn, at the end of which your choices are an easy run down the Baciver valley through the trees or sticking to the supersteep main piste. The piste ends by crossing a wooden bridge over the Malo ("bad") river before you reach the base station of the chairlift back up.

Two hours and 18 minutes of black

The run is located in Baqueira's Cara Norte ("north face") sector where much of the best freeride terrain is also located, although not marked on the maps. It's best to hire a guide and check the avalanche risk with ski patrol to enjoy all that.

The Luis Arias trail is also included in one of the three "ski safari" routes promoted by the resort for novice, intermediate, and expert skiers. The run comes toward the end of the black safari for experts, a run-by-run description of which can be found on the resort's website in English. The black route is precisely 14.3 miles (23.11km) long, incorporates 14,655ft (4,468.1m) of vertical descent and will take two hours and 18 minutes to complete if you don't stop and there's no queue for any lift. It's good to be precise about these things!

The online guide has lots of practical advice, too, beginning with top tips to be prepared for your trip around the slopes. "Skis well waxed? Binding adjusted to the right point? Helmet on? Glasses on? Zips done up? ... " Then we're off to take the high-speed four-seat Mirador lift to begin our safari. "Watch out for beginners as you cross the ski-school area ... "

Probably the most remarked-upon aspect of the resort by visitors is just how friendly the locals are, easily overcoming any language barriers that may come about from the complex combination of a local Aranes district dialect, the Catalan regional language, and then the French and Spanish influences that all merge together here. And that is why visitors love Baqueira Beret—along with its skiing, its scenery, its great food and, of course, that royal recommendation.

Fact file Luis Arias

IN SHORT: Snowier, sunnier, and sometimes steeper than the Alps or Rockies, Baqueira Beret comes with royal approval

TOUGHNESS:
☠☠☠

FEAR FACTOR:
☠☠☠

VERTICAL: 8,095–6,107ft (2,468–1,862m) (1,988ft/606m vertical)

AVERAGE TIME:
3 mins, 28 secs

LENGTH OF RUN:
2,624yds (2,407m)

ACCESS:
Jorge Jordana chairlift

BEST TIME: All season, due to its north-oriented face

AVALANCHE KIT:
Nonessential

ALTITUDE RANGE: 4,920–8,233ft (1,500–2,510m) (3,313ft/1,010m vertical)

SKIABLE AREA:
74.4 miles (120km)

RUNS: 72

LIFTS: 33

WEB: baqueira.es

GETTING THERE: Toulouse (102.3 miles/165km), Barcelona (210.8 miles/340km)

SPAIN

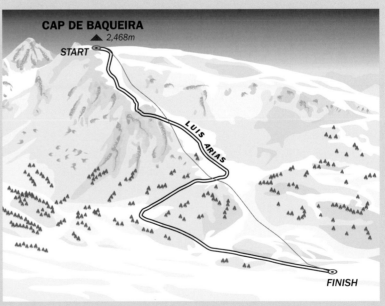

CAP DE BAQUEIRA
▲ 2,468m
START

LUIS ARIAS

FINISH

Pic du Midi
Pyrenees, France
8,200ft (2,500m)

A long-standing cult destination, the Pic du Midi blows apart the misconception of the Pyrenees, among some, as a rather tame destination best suited to beginner- and intermediate-level skiers. In fact, the Pic du Midi de Bigorre (to give it its full title) is a relatively unique proposition in world skiing. There are other ski runs around the world that are crowned by an astronomical observatory (one thinks of Mauna Kea in Hawaii, at the top of a 33,456-ft (10,200-m) vertical, the world's biggest—such a shame that only the first few hundred feet are ever snow covered and the bottom three-fifths are under the Pacific anyway). But few others have cable-car access and winter snow, and those that do either have no skiing or rather less inspiring descents.

And indeed the Pic du Midi formerly had no skiing, officially, unless you chose to climb up yourself. But the descent of up to 6,232 vertical feet (1,900m) from the 9,437-ft (2,877-m) observatory was well known to ski mountaineers and in the late 1990s, as finance for the observatory was running thin, a decision was made to look at how revenue could be derived from tourism.

Eventually in 2002, after consultation with other resorts famed for their more extreme skiing including Chamonix and La Grave, the decision was made to allow skiing and boarding from the top of the brand new cable car (the previous one had been installed nearly 50 years before). However, this was to be allowed only when accompanied by a guide, when fully equipped for avalanche and other dangers and having signed a disclaimer at the ticket office before ascending. In 2006 the requirement to ski with a guide was relaxed, although it remains highly recommended.

A peak with a view

On a clear day, the views from the Pic du Midi, the highest lift-served point in the Pyrenees, are truly stunning. There are up to 186 miles (300km) of mountain peaks in view, and it is imperative that you stay a while and take in the 360-degree panorama. Indeed, in clear conditions, the night sky above is equally stunning—NASA installed their own telescope here in 1964 to map the surface of the moon ahead of the Apollo missions. It is possible to stay in original (but fully modernized) accommodation at the observatory overnight—where there are 15 bedrooms with a capacity of up to 27 people that feature raised beds to admire the view of the Pyrenees—and then ski down the next morning.

There's also a museum, a store, a champagne bar, and a traditional restaurant at the summit, and the majority of the 110,000-plus people visiting the observatory each year do so to visit these attractions, then take the lift back down. You'll have the skiing pretty much to yourself.

So, to the slopes! The Pic du Midi de Bigorre is a perfect pyramid and towers more than 6,560 vertical feet (2,000m) above the Lannemezan plateau. As with the Vallée Blanche, there's a classic route down and many variations thereupon, including longer and steeper options.

The classic route leads you down toward the resort of Barèges, over 3,280 vertical feet (1,000m) below, with those longer runs (subject to conditions) including the Coume Peak run (4,920ft/1,500m) or the Combe de l'Ours (which translates as "The Valley of the Bear") that takes you down some 5,576 vertical feet (1,700m) and takes around four hours to complete. Both of these routes end up in the little hamlet of Artigues. A shuttle bus, the *navette de freeriders*, will take you back to La Mongie from Artigues.

The classic run begins with a very short and gentle hike up to the sometimes-windswept peak before starting your descent. If it was groomed and graded, this might be a black-gradient slope with those magnificent vistas still in front of you, before it drops into vast, wide, sweeping, powder-filled valleys between rocky buttresses. In normal conditions a good off-piste skier can cope with these and indeed obtain maximum powder pleasure from them.

For the most extreme, there are options *en route* including the infamous northeast face, which narrows to a 164-ft (50-m) cliff that has a ribbon of snow a little more than a ski's width to negotiate.

Sign on the dotted line

Whether you make it a day trip or have made a night of it (or go somewhere between the two and take one of the springtime sunset descents offered at up to 7.30 p.m. on selected dates), you will have signed that legal document. It's in French, but there are translations in English, German, and Spanish of what you're agreeing to—that you've checked the weather and snow reports posted in La Mongie ticket office and cable-car station, that you know what you're taking on, and are up to the task, that you're fully equipped (with transceiver, probe, rope, crampons, ice axe, shovel, etc.) and that you take responsibility for any under 18-year-olds with you.

" THE SLOPES CAN BE CLOSED FOR WEEKS ON END IF THERE'S TOO MUCH SNOW AND THE AVALANCHE RISK TOO HIGH. "

LEFT: Famed for its deep powder and spectacular views, legally you must be properly equipped and skilled to tackle this kind of unpatroled, unprepared off-piste terrain before you're allowed to ride the slopes of Pic du Midi.
RIGHT: Magnificent views open out below you as you descend the 6,232 vertical off-piste feet (1,900m) from the Pic du Midi, at nearly 9,840ft (3,000m) the highest lift-served point in the Pyrenees.

La Mongie and Barèges are conventional and interconnected ski areas that share the Grand Tourmalet ski area and 62 miles (100km) of groomed piste between them. A special, unlimited off-piste ski pass covers your Pic du Midi ascent, although the guiding is, of course, extra. But it does mean Pic du Midi can be an excursion during a week's stay in the region.

At your own peril

Apart from trying to ensure common sense on the part of skiers and boarders taking to these unpatroled slopes to minimize the danger of accidents, the site operators also want to minimize their own danger of financial liability if an accident does happen. But although they highlight the unpatroled, unprepared, and nonavalanche-secured nature of the skiing here, the authorities do take care and the slopes can be closed for weeks on end if there's too much snow and the avalanche risk too high, or too little. Time your visit right, however, and this truly is one of the greatest descents on earth.

Fact file Pic du Midi

IN SHORT: The most spectacular descent in the Pyrenees

TOUGHNESS:
☠☠☠

FEAR FACTOR:
☠☠☠

VERTICAL: 9,437–3,205ft (2,877–977m) (6,232ft/1,900m vertical)

AVERAGE TIME: Four hours

LENGTH OF RUN: 3.1 miles (5km)

ACCESS: Cable car

BEST TIME: Usually springtime

AVALANCHE KIT: Essential

ALTITUDE RANGE: 4,592–9,437ft (1,400–2,877m) (Barèges/La Mongie)

SKIABLE AREA: 62 miles (100km) (Barèges/La Mongie)

RUNS: 69 (Barèges/La Mongie)

LIFTS: 40 (Barèges/La Mongie)

WEB: picdumidi.com horspistes.fr

GETTING THERE: Ossun/Tarbes/Lourdes (27.9 miles/45km)

FRANCE

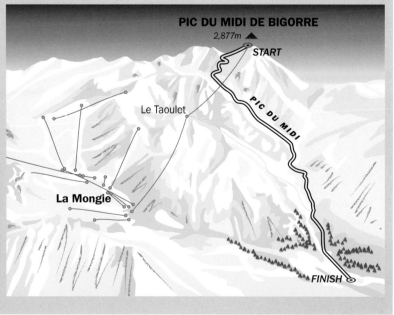

PIC DU MIDI DE BIGORRE
2,877m ▲
START

Le Taoulet

PIC DU MIDI

La Mongie

FINISH

Bellecôte
La Plagne, France
10,660ft (3,250m)

The scale of the giant Paradiski region that links the ski areas of La Plagne, Peisey Vallandry, and Les Arcs via the Vanoise Express double-decker cable car, popularly regarded as the third-largest ski region in the world with more than 24,710 acres (10,000ha) of skiable terrain, is such that there will always be debate about the most challenging, the most awe-inspiring descent. There are certainly plenty of people on the hunt for it—La Plagne officially receives more skiers each winter (over two million) than any of the world's other 5,000-plus ski areas.

However, the vast majority of these skiing and boarding millions are here for the hundreds of miles of groomed piste, much of it intermediate cruising, and La Plagne's more enticing freeride terrain for experts—which most consider among the world's best—tends to be overlooked behind this "family-friendly" reputation.

In fact the Paradiski region has almost 40 marked black trails, the most challenging of which include the 2.17-mile- (3.5-km-) long Le Rochu piste. But it's what's off the marked pistes altogether that's particularly exciting for serious skiers and boarders, and for those who know and love La Plagne's steeps, the descent that receives the most rave reviews, time and time again, is the (up to) 6,560 vertical-foot (2,000-m), off-piste route down the north face of the Bellecôte right to the village of Les Lanches (Nancroix) in the valley below.

Depending on where you are based in this huge resort with its ten separate base villages, it can be a trek up to the 10,660-ft (3,250-m) summit of the Bellecôte glacier. It is the highest lift-accessible point in the entire Paradiski region, with its year-round snow cover that meant it was once open for summer skiing. Even from Belle Plagne (6,724ft/2,050m), the closest, it's a three-stage gondola ride, beginning with the Roche di Mio lift, then moving on to the lift that first opened in 1978 and is named after the peak. On a good day, the trip from Plagne Bellecôte to this highest lift-served point of the ski resort takes about 40 minutes; longer from the resort's other villages or even across the Vanoise Express double-decker cable car that makes the link from Les Arcs and Peisey Vallandry. At the end of the day it can also provide the

easiest route back to La Plagne from the base of the Face Nord de Bellecôte, depending on which route you follow down.

Whichever way you come, looking out of your cabin on the final stage you can see the impressive slopes that await you, and once you reach the summit ridge at the top after taking the traverse chairlift across, some of the many off-piste descent options are visible.

Petit Face Nord

There are many routes down from the 3.72-mile- (6-km-) long ridge, and a guide is advisable for all. The most commonly taken route is the optimistically named "easiest" or Petit Face Nord, which begins with a short ski traverse around the shoulder onto the Petit Face before your descent into the least demanding of the couloirs to skier's left of the summit, some 656ft (200m) higher. The whole area is prone to enormous avalanches that are vented down through the couloirs and it is frequently closed in a "typical" season because of that.

Getting started is relatively easy, but finding the right way through the complex flow of the landscape as you descend is where your guide's experience will be invaluable. Indeed, it would be foolhardy and potentially fatal to attempt this run without a guide.

After leaving the shoulder there are many options on this wide face, but the most commonly used route passes through a fairly steep (but wide) 35-degree couloir, before the slope opens up and you have time to catch your breath and take a look at the magnificent cirque formed by the mountain face.

The rest of the descent is more gentle, with the great powder that's a key attraction at the top of the run hopefully continuing for all or at least most of the descent as you cruise down through unspoilt countryside into the Ponthurin valley and toward the treeline. You could be in a different world, and you will quickly forget that you have just left a ski resort that's visited by millions of people each winter. The last third of the run is through the trees, and the final section of this route takes you down into the river valley joining the alternative exit for the various other couloirs starting high on the north face. Either continuing on the left bank or crossing the river you will arrive at the Fer à Cheval restaurant, a welcome sight after a long descent. There are no lifts at the bottom, but a free bus will take you back to the lift network.

RIGHT: The north face of Bellecôte delivers some of the planet's steepest, deepest and, without a guide, potentially most dangerous terrain. Recent landslides mean the middle section now includes a variety of sharp rocks that must also be negotiated.

Rocks, cliffs, and 50-plus degrees

If the "easy route" isn't for you, then the Vallençant couloir, which offers around 3,772ft (1,150m) of vertical descent, may suit you better. For the first 656ft (200m) this pitches at an exceptionally steep 50-plus degrees, and with rocks and cliffs below, a fall doesn't bear thinking about. After that the run becomes a more manageable (but still seriously steep) 35–40-degree gradient hemmed in by cliffs on most sides all the way to meadows below.

Another famous (and slightly less intimidating) option, the Couloir des Canadiens—named after a group of Canadians who first skied it in the 1950s—is a further choice. Used for freeride competitions in the past, the angle is a slightly less intimidating 45 degrees at the ridge entry point directly into a narrow couloir normally below a large cornice, with the couloir becoming easier the lower you go.

The couloir is much longer and wider than most, for added pleasure, but following recent landslides, a serious 35–40-degree middle section with sharp rocks some 1,312ft (400m) below the entry point must also be

ABOVE: A series of lifts climb across one of the world's largest and highest ski areas to provide access to the north face, where you'll go off the map and discover some of the steepest runs (up to 40-degree gradient), hemmed in by cliffs on both sides.

negotiated before the route opens out into a wider couloir and joins the broad snow fields below.

At least a dozen other options are possible, most with similarly challenging and very steep starts where falling is not recommended. These are followed by other hazards for those who don't know the routes intimately, including couloirs ending in cliffs, slopes with glacial seracs falling away on one side, and even the springtime option for one route of falling into a stream and getting swept down under the snow. Some, however, are easier and generally agreed to be "not much worse than your average black run, only off-piste." But to find the best route for your ability, and the safest route whatever your ability, there are few ski runs in the world where a local guide is more essential.

Fact file **Bellecôte**

IN SHORT: A 50-plus degrees couloir prone to enormous avalanches—hence frequently closed

TOUGHNESS:
☠☠☠☠

FEAR FACTOR:
☠☠☠☠

VERTICAL: 10,332–4,920ft (3,150–1,500m) (5,412ft/1,650m vertical)

AVERAGE TIME: 30 minutes to two hours

LENGTH OF RUN: 2.4–3.1 miles (4–5km)

ACCESS: Gondola lift

BEST TIME: January–April

AVALANCHE KIT: Essential

ALTITUDE RANGE: 4,100–10,660ft (1,250–3,250m)

SKIABLE AREA: 139.5 miles (225km) (Paradiski: 263.5 miles/425km)

RUNS: 130 (Paradiski: 236)

LIFTS: 80 (Paradiski: 135)

WEB: la-plagne.com paradiski.com

GETTING THERE: Geneva (92.4 miles/ 149km)

FRANCE

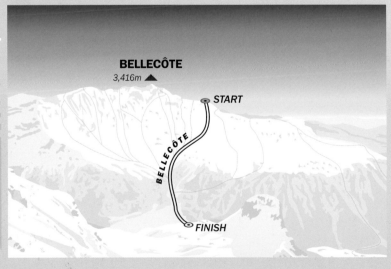

BELLECÔTE
3,416m ▲

START

BELLECÔTE

FINISH

Sarenne
Alpe d'Huez, France
10,922ft (3,330m)

A world of eternal snow, the top of the Alpe d'Huez ski area is among the highest in France, opening up some of the biggest verticals and longest runs in existence. It is also home to the official longest black run on earth, Sarenne.

"The world's longest black run" is a title that can send mixed messages. The obvious attraction is an enduring, challenging descent beyond all others; the more negative connotation is that stretching a black run's length out has to mean less of a gradient. Even if the Sarenne run at Alpe d'Huez is in the world top ten for lift-served vertical descents of around 6,560ft (2,000m), skiing for 9.9 miles (16km) on a run, even with that vertical, gives an average gradient of little more than ten percent—equating to a blue grade at most resorts. In fact, the 9.9-mile- (16-km-) long run is not only the longest black run but also the longest marked run of any kind.

The explanation of the grading is that the Sarenne is a run of two halves, the upper half plummeting away to fully deserve its black title, the lower section a fairly flat trail that's more green or blue than anything to balance the black. Some resorts would, of course, grade the two halves of the run differently—but in defense of Alpe d'Huez, you do need to take the steep stretch to reach the flat, so it does make some sense.

You reach the top of the run via the Pic Blanc cable car, which lifts you to a lofty 109,22ft (3,330m), a spot from which there are both magnificent 360-degree views across the mostly lower peaks that surround you (for that true "on top of the world" feeling) and a plethora of pisted and unpisted expert-level terrain, the latter best explored with a guide. This is also glacier territory; not many years ago, the Sarenne glacier was open for summer skiing (and opened again as recently as 2013 after an exceptionally snowy spring).

Because of its reputation, the Sarenne run is usually the most popular and busiest way down, although early morning and lunchtime are often quieter than mid-morning and afternoon.

Steep and icy moguls

The upper section is the steepest and most challenging of the whole run and is rarely groomed, so moguls build up with all the traffic. To add to the challenge, they're often icy at this altitude if there's been no fresh snow for a while. It is quite wide, however, so there is plenty of space to pick your route.

If you really don't like steep, icy moguls, they can be avoided by taking the Marmottes 3 gondola and joining the run a little way below. Although where's the fun in that, and you won't be able to say that you did it top to bottom. Once past those challenging first few hundred feet, the run may still not have much grooming because of the rock bands and other natural hazards that break up the upper section, and which you may need to ski around.

RIGHT: The Sarenne run at Alpe d'Huez presents a mixture of challenging terrain and fast cruising, but the views as you descend remain consistently spectacular.

As you descend further, one of the great rewards of this descent—besides the views over toward Les Deux Alpes and La Grave's ski area on La Meije—is that you find yourself far away from other lifts, other runs, and hopefully other skiers. The magnificent views, however, stay with you—a kind of microcosm of the Vallée Blanche experience.

There can be challenges: narrower sections sometimes have sheet ice, and if the sun that hits this slope full-on has thawed it a little, you may have to watch out for rocks.

Le Tunnel

Almost all of the run lies above the treeline and the upper sections run relatively straight down before the slope swings to skier's left and into the Gorges de Sarenne—a fun feature, but also a rather flat one (boarders beware: the black-level challenge here is to keep moving on the final 3.1 or 3.7 miles (5–6km) of fairly level piste). At the bottom as the treeline is finally reached, the Alpauris chairlift is waiting to whisk you back up toward Alpe d'Huez at 6,101ft (1,860m) above.

ABOVE: The remarkable Pic Blanc cable car accesses year-round glacier slopes and takes you to the top of the Sarenne descent.

The lack of great challenge in Sarenne will no doubt lead some to question why we have included it in this book, pointing perhaps instead to the excellent off-piste descents for which Alpe d'Huez has a reputation, as do its neighbors Les Deux Alpes and La Grave. On the groomed pistes there are greater challenges, too, including the run directly beneath the Pic Blanc cable car which is steep, often mogulled, and awkward to access from the long tunnel you ski through to reach it, hence its name of Le Tunnel. So the advice is that, when in Alpe d'Huez, try all these delights, but Sarenne is in the book because as "the world's longest black run"—rightly or wrongly so designated—it probably ought to be.

Even if you disagree with the rating and the inclusion, you can at least enjoy the view and the wonderful feeling of isolation that the Sarenne piste delivers. Until you reach the bottom of the run, where a wonderful little mountain restaurant awaits with a welcoming beer.

Fact file Sarenne

IN SHORT: The longest black run in the world: it speaks for itself, or does it?

TOUGHNESS:
☠☠☠

FEAR FACTOR:
☠☠☠

VERTICAL:
10,922–4,362ft
(3,330–1,330m)

AVERAGE TIME:
15 minutes or longer

LENGTH OF RUN:
9.9 miles (16km)

ACCESS: Pic Blanc cable car

BEST TIME:
December–April

AVALANCHE KIT:
Nonessential

ALTITUDE RANGE: 3,608–10,922ft (1,100–3,330m)

SKIABLE AREA:
48.8 miles (240km)

RUNS: 131

LIFTS: 73

WEB:
alpedhuez.com

GETTING THERE: Grenoble (61.4 miles/99km), Lyon (93 miles/150km)

FRANCE

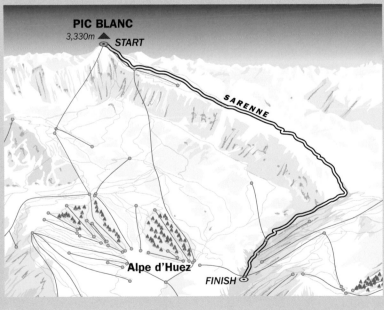

PIC BLANC
3,330m ▲ START

SARENNE

Alpe d'Huez

FINISH

Face de Bellevarde
Val d'Isère, France
11,644ft (3,550m)

The number of ski areas that have hosted Alpine Skiing World Cup events over the decades may total more than 100. Less than 30 have hosted Alpine Skiing World Championships over the 80-plus years they've been around, and fewer still have been Winter Olympic venues. But how many resorts have staged all three? Of the thousands of ski areas around the world you can count them on one hand, and the Face de Bellevarde has seen World Cup, World Championship, and Olympic winners crowned.

The story goes that, one day in the late 1980s, the great Jean Claude Killy, the triple champion from the 1968 Grenoble Olympics, charged with organizing the next French-hosted games in Albertville in 1992, had an epiphany. Killy had been trying to determine where the blue-ribbon downhill races should take place at the '92 Games—having at his disposal many of the world's top ski resorts in the French Savoie region. It came to him that the only place to provide the challenge and the excitement worthy of the Games was the Face de Bellevarde, and nowhere else would do.

ABOVE: A precipitous descent on the Face de Bellevarde rewards you with a view of Val d'Isère lying below. It's not quite as "aerial" as this one—although it is not far off.

At the time, Bellevarde was not a competition slope. It had hosted the French Championships of 1952 and was famous mostly for the number of skiers that had crashed off the course on that occasion. By the 1980s it was famous as an off-piste gem, and Killy's decision did not initially appear an auspicious one.

Undeterred by the popular perception of the unsuitability of the Face de Bellevarde for racing in the modern era, Killy contacted his friend Bernhard Russi, the Swiss winner of the downhill at the 1972 Sapporo Olympics in Japan, and they met on the Face to assess its possibilities.

The two men discussed the realities of building on the mountainside. Was it presumptuous to imagine that a showpiece event such as the downhill could be organized on it? Could a modern course be designed on it? History shows that their decision was "Yes," and that it was the correct conclusion. After Olympics and World Championships, the run still hosts World Cup racing each December—the first downhill races in the Alps each season on the two weekends before Christmas, thanks to the snowsure altitude of the Face.

Russi's plan was that the course must be technical and attractive enough to appeal to racers, but also to the public and the television companies needing strong images of key sections. The course was designed so that 80 percent of it was visible to spectators waiting at the base, and so that the bottom extends right the way into the heart of the resort—helping to create a sensational atmosphere on race day from top to bottom. Unusually in World Cup racing, racers can also see and hear the fans at the base, nearly 3,280 vertical feet (1,000m) below, as they set off.

So what have Messrs Killy and Russi designed for those of us unable to complete our descent in the one minute, 50.37 seconds that the Austrian Patrick Ortlieb managed in order to win the 1992 Olympic gold, five-hundredths of a second ahead of French champion Frank Piccard; nor even the two minutes, 7.01 seconds that Canadian John Kucera took to win the 2009 Alpine World Championships gold? (Kucera's time was slower, as the International Ski Federation (FIS) safety rules changed in 1992 and two large bends were added to the course to slow the racers down a little).

While criticized by some hardcore skiers for not being as steep as its reputation implies (the average pitch is 31.2 percent), the Face de Bellevarde is popularly acknowledged as a true black run, and with the steepness of its pitch varying from five to 71 percent, it is a technical course that keeps you on your toes from start to finish.

3,280 vertical feet (1,000m) of moguls

The run is accessed by a superb, high-speed Doppelmayr gondola, installed for a mere €15 million back in 2002, which whisks you directly from the village to the top of the run. Around the top of the mountain, the run then curves rather benignly (do not be deceived) before it begins to plummet down the east-facing slope.

Much of the challenge of the Face de Bellevarde for the nonracer relies upon conditions when you visit. It is not the steepest run in the Espace Killy, the giant ski region that links Tignes and Val d'Isère, but its notoriety makes it one of the most popular, with the consequence that you may have to negotiate a crowded slope, or else you will find that thousands of skiers have polished the slope to ice. It is not unusual for the entire Face to be carved into nearly 3,280 vertical feet (1,000m) of moguls. If you do face such a challenge to your knees and your stamina, you do at least have the excuse that you simply must stop halfway down to take in the magnificent views across the valley to the Solaise ski area.

But hit it on a quieter day, perhaps with a little fresh snow, and you can fly down—perhaps not quite as quickly as the world's best, but certainly as fast as you safely dare.

On a powder day, the Face de Bellevarde takes on a whole extra dimension of challenge and pleasure.

Fact file Face de Bellevarde

IN SHORT: One of the world's greatest runs, conceived by one of the world's greatest skiers and then designed by another

TOUGHNESS:
☠☠☠

FEAR FACTOR:
☠☠☠

VERTICAL: 9,207–6,061ft (2,807–1,848m) (3,146ft/959m vertical)

AVERAGE TIME: Two minutes (but probably longer for you and me)

LENGTH OF RUN: 3,257yds (2,988m)

ACCESS: Olympique lift

BEST TIME: January–May

AVALANCHE KIT: Nonessential

ALTITUDE RANGE: 5,084–11,644ft (1,550–3,550m)

SKIABLE AREA: 186 miles (300km)

RUNS: 154

LIFTS: 90

WEB: valdisere.com

GETTING THERE: Geneva (111.6 miles/180km), Chambéry (80.6 miles/130km), Lyon (136.4 miles/220km)

LA GRANDE MOTTE
3,550m ▲

START

FACE DE BELLEVARDE

FINISH

FRANCE

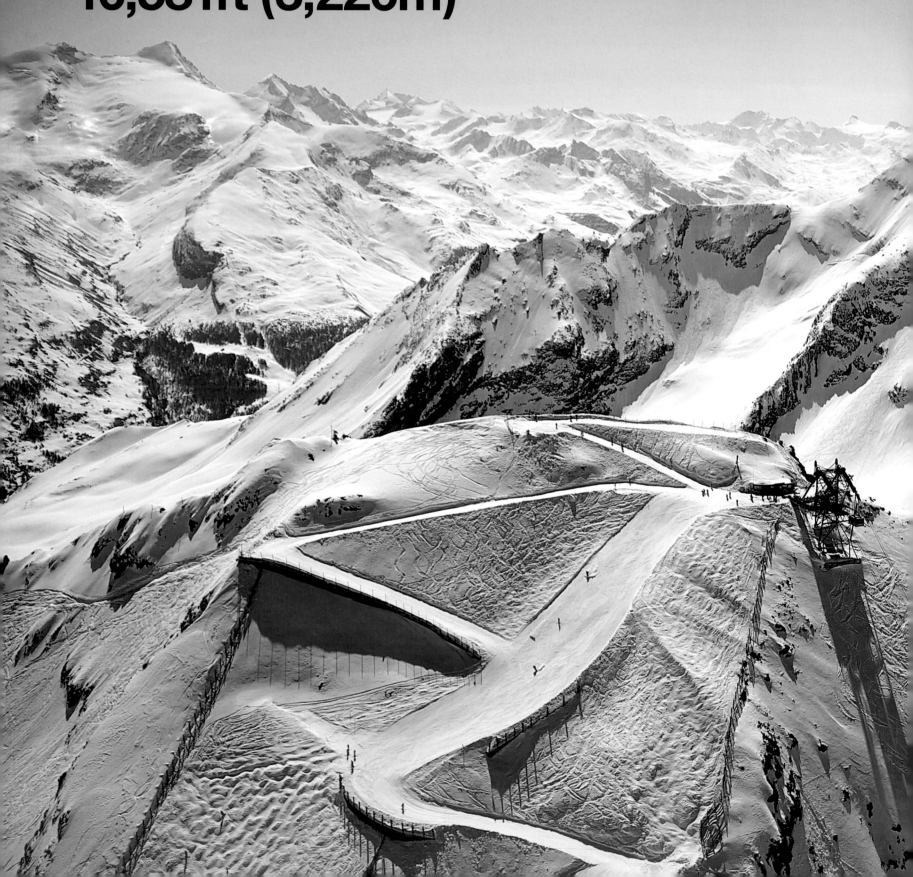

Aiguille Rouge
Les Arcs, France
10,581ft (3,226m)

The Paradiski ski area, of which Les Arcs forms a major part, is one of the world's three largest, with one of the planet's biggest lift-served verticals.

A sign at the bottom of the Aiguille Rouge cable car has, for many decades, warned the inexperienced skier or boarder that there is no easy way down from the 10,581-ft (3,226-m) summit. As you ascend, you can look down over a series of serious couloirs that visually underline what that sign is telling you.

The Aiguille Rouge is the highest peak on the Les Arcs side of the giant Paradiski region that links the resort—famed for introducing cool new snow sports to the world (monoboarding and something a lot like snowboarding, just before Jake Burton came along, were both big here), and filming them in cult movies such as *Apocalypse Snow*—to neighboring giant area La Plagne and smaller Peisey-Vallandry, to create one of the world's five largest ski areas.

There is, in fact, a wide, glorious red run carving its way across the front of the mountain, high above the treeline, below the lift, but the main attractions here are the numerous black runs and the off-piste potential. In particular, there is one of the greatest lift-served descents you can find, that takes you 4.3 miles (7km) down its 6,642ft (2,025m) of vertical descent—one of the planet's ten biggest.

It's particularly worth noting the amount of vertical you descend for the length of run. Compare this to "the longest black run in the world" (Sarenne in Alpe d'Huez) at 10 miles (16km) over 7,314 vertical feet (2,230m)—in other words more than twice as long for only 672ft (205m) more vertical—and even the novice mathematician can calculate that this descent down to the little village of Villaroger must be about twice as steep.

The Aiguille Rouge run

If your jaw is not already dropping from the stats, wait for the view from the top. As with many of the long runs described in this book, the 360-degree views from the top of this lift, on a good day, are spectacular and worth taking some time to appreciate before you start

ABOVE: For a variation on the main descent, there are gullies and couloirs to drop into off parts of the Aiguille Rouge run.

your descent. A viewing table tells you that on a clear day you are seeing the Grande Casse, the Grand Motte crowning Tignes, Mont Pourri, and, further off, Mont Blanc and summits over the border in Italy.

Luckily, this delay in your departure also makes sense for ensuring that the run is fairly empty when you start your descent, as most of the 70 other people in the cable car will race straight off, trying not to collide with each other.

The piste is officially known as "the Aiguille Rouge run," and has both black and red options for most of its great length. Some good skiers argue that some of the black sections are overrated. But be that as it may, the first few hundred feet of the very top black section are the steepest and can be challenging, particularly in icy conditions when a narrow part of the piste can prove tricky. Ensure you take the black, not the red option, and around 328ft (100m) down there's often a choice of moguls to the right or a smoother, red slope to the left, depending on your preference.

In the lower half of the black-graded section, a number of still-steeper pistes plunge off to skier's left and down to Arc 2000, most more highly regarded by those seeking powder or steeps than the Aiguille Rouge run itself. Runs such as the black Genepy and Combe pistes will tempt you off your target and you are forgiven, if conditions are pristine, if you opt to drop down onto them (or if a guide takes you to the powder in between) and do another lap around (using the Varet gondola to return to the base of the Aiguille Rouge cable car); alternatively, you could leave them for later in the day. An earlier turn along the start of the red Arandelieres run near the top gives the additional option of skiing the black Robert Blanc couloir, named after the resort's founder and often gorged with snow.

Stay on course

Be sure you have checked snow conditions before attempting any of these, however. The cable car will close when conditions are extremely bad, to the annoyance of the foolhardy determined to ski the off-piste areas having made the trip, but people have died having insisted on skiing areas when piste patrol has closed them.

Staying on course and avoiding these tantalizing distractions, you reach the treeline just as the terrain turns from black to red and you can relax into a more high-speed cruising pattern. The trail moves past a protected nature area on skier's right as you descend toward the valley.

Villaroger is a quiet village with two restaurants in which to order a celebratory beer. A couple of successive chairlifts take you back up to the lift network. Take a couple more after that and you're back at the base station of that famous cable car, ready to go again. The downside of that plan is that long queues sometimes develop for the cable car; it's best to get up there first thing to avoid that danger and enjoy the descent in the morning sunshine.

For the seriously obsessed, if conditions are good you can, in fact, ski on down another 410 vertical feet (125m), but you'd need to hike back up from the base in order to say you'd managed 7,216ft (2,200m) of vertical descent. That might be overdoing it just a tad.

ABOVE: The black Genepy and Combe pistes, down toward Arc 2000 on the lower half of the black-graded section, will look a more tempting route to those seeking powder.

Fact file Aiguille Rouge

IN SHORT: There is no easy way down from the 10,581-ft (3,226-m) summit

TOUGHNESS: ☠☠☠

FEAR FACTOR: ☠☠☠

VERTICAL: 10,581–3,936ft (3,226–1,200m) (6,645ft/2,026m vertical)

AVERAGE TIME: 45 mins

LENGTH OF RUN: 4.3 miles (7km)

ACCESS: Aiguille Rouge cable car, Arc 2000

BEST TIME: February onward for the best sunshine and snow, as some parts of this ski run are largely in the shade before this

AVALANCHE KIT: Minimal

ALTITUDE RANGE: 3,936–10,581ft (1,200–3,226m)

SKIABLE AREA: 124 miles (200km) (Paradiski 263.5 miles/425km)

RUNS: 106 (Paradiski 236)

LIFTS: 52 (Paradiski 135)

WEB: lesarcs.com paradiski.com facebook.com/LesArcsWinter

GETTING THERE: Geneva or Lyon 93 miles (150km); Bourg St Maurice below Les Arcs direct by Eurostar from London

FRANCE

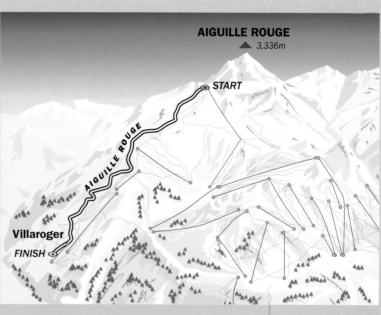

AIGUILLE ROUGE
▲ 3,336m

START

AIGUILLE ROUGE

Villaroger
FINISH

La Vallée Blanche
Chamonix, France
12,602ft (3,842m)

❝ YOU SUDDENLY FIND YOURSELF EXPOSED ON AN ICY RIDGE WITH INCREASINGLY STEEPER SLOPES FALLING AWAY ON EITHER SIDE. IF YOU SLIP, IT'S A FAIRLY DIRECT NONSTOP DESCENT OF SEVERAL THOUSAND FEET. ❞

The stats are impressive. With a peak of 12,602ft (3,842m), Europe's second highest lift-served point, and descending a total of 9,184 vertical feet (2,800m), the world's longest possible lift-served descent, it's no surprise that the Vallée Blanche is the "must do" descent for any serious skier or boarder. Indeed, an estimated 80,000 tackle the (up to) 13.6-mile (22-km) off-piste itinerary every season.

The run itself is spectacular. Descending Géant, Tacul, and the Mer de Glace glaciers and surrounded by mighty peaks including the Aiguille du Midi, Mont Blanc, Grand Flambeau, Pointe Helbronner, and Dent du Géant, this is a pristine glacier environment that feels a million miles from the rest of humanity—a very different, very special descent for most skiers and worthy of its reputation.

But is it challenging? That depends to an extent on the route that you take. The classic descent, used by the majority, is relatively easy in terms of gradient; you slide along gentle glacier slopes, which might equate to a blue or a red run if it were a groomed piste.

The main challenge is an unusual one for regular recreational skiers. It comes from the tricky access via the infamous arête and the danger of death posed by glacial crevasses (alas, the fate of one or two people virtually every season). Then for the least fit, stamina is required to ski ungroomed terrain for, usually, three to four hours. Even pristine powder can become wearisome over very long, fairly flat descents; hard-packed, wind-blown slab with no fresh cover and clattering skis or board can be exhausting. If you can cope with all that, intermediate-standard skiers can tackle the route, although more experienced skiers are likely to enjoy it more.

If you do require additional challenge, there are alternatives to that classic route (described as "glacier sightseeing on skis" by the distinguished ski travel writer, Adam Ruck) that add to the difficulty and the variety of the terrain. The Grand Envers du Plan, for example, regarded as the most beautiful and the most difficult ski route of all the Vallée Blanche variations, is for expert skiers only, who'll need to ensure they stay on their feet descending gradients of up to 45 degrees.

Whichever route you take, we all start the same way: by hiring a guide to make sure the run is enjoyable and safe. These can be booked via the Bureau des Guides (chamonix-guides.com), which charges a flat rate for up to six people.

The next step is the vertigo-inducing, two-stage cable-car ascent of some 9,184 vertical feet (2,800m) from central Chamonix to the start of the descent via the Aiguille du Midi cable car. First envisaged in 1905 by two Swiss engineers, this remarkable lift, which ascends first to the Plan de l'Aiguille—7,5444ft (2,300m)—and then on across the Pélerins glacier and up the north face of the Aiguille du Midi, was finally completed in 1955 and was fully renovated in the 1990s. The great height and rapid ascent can be problematic for some people and it's important to acclimatize before tackling the Vallée Blanche; don't try it on your first day in Chamonix.

A frightening challenge

The top station ends at 12,646ft (3,800m), with a final 138-ft (42-m) vertigo-inducing elevator ride up through the rock; it is an attraction in its own right and has recently undergone a multimillion euro upgrade. On a clear day, you can see across to the Swiss Alps and the Matterhorn; this is also the closest point to the summit of Mont Blanc, you can reach without climbing it.

A clear day following some fresh snowfall is also ideal for enjoying the Vallée Blanche—particularly those first few minutes, when you exit the protection of the cable-car's top station, built to withstand extreme weather, and you suddenly find yourself exposed on an icy ridge with increasingly steeper slopes falling away on either side. If you slip, it's a nonstop descent of several thousand feet.

For many people this arête, which you edge down for several hundred feet from the cable-car station to the start of the ski run, is the most frightening part of the entire Vallée Blanche. There is a rope to cling onto, leading along the length of the arête, but it's still a challenge when you're carrying your skis or board and trying to balance on gently sloping ice. Some opt for crampons or wear profile-soled ski boots, and groups are usually roped together by their guides. There is some debate over whether skiers or boarders have an advantage on the arête; snowboarding boots have slightly better grip, but if the wind is whipping around then holding on to a snowboard can be trickier than skis. One option is to attach skis to a backsack, leaving your hands free. Boarders are advised to take poles for the descent, to help on the flatter sections.

So after all that preparation and feats of endurance, the actual run may seem like an afterthought. There's a great feeling of joy and

camaraderie as you stand at the start of the longest ski run of your life, surrounded by nature's majesty.

The terrain is so vast that even the several thousand visitors it attracts each day are quickly dispersed; you may see few others on your run down. Most people follow the main route, which essentially follows the valley floor above glaciers, turning first toward Italy and passing below the Helbronner gondola. Continuing to the Col du Midi beneath the rocky Gros Rognon on the left and traversing toward the cliffs of the Mont Blanc du Tacul, you're surrounded by breathtaking glacier scenery.

As you are skiing on a glacier, at times on snow bridges over crevasses, it is wise to stay on the tracks left by preceding skiers and, of course, to follow your guide's route advice. The key point to skiing the Vallée Blanche is never to overtake the guide. Anybody skiing the Vallée Blanche needs to be in control and capable of stopping when necessary. In 1955, Louis Lachenal, who had been the first man to climb above 26,240ft (8,000m), fell through a snow bridge on the Vallée Blanche to his death in a glacial crevasse; it can happen to anyone.

Most people bring lunch with them, but you can reserve a space at the Refuge du Requin at 8,252ft (2,516m), which faces the Séracs du Géant. The next section, over the wide Mer de Glace, is relatively green/blue in gradient: a fairly flat section with great views of the Drus summits.

There is some debate among the statistically obsessed as to just how big a vertical the Vallée Blanche really is and whether, in practical terms, several other resorts, including Verbier, Zermatt, and Val Thorens, can offer bigger constant descents if conditions are right. The actual top of the run, after the arête, has been put at 12,234ft (3,730m), some 367 vertical feet (112m) less than the popularly quoted figure, and in any case the full vertical cannot be skied in one go—perhaps nearer 6,888ft (2,100m) can. But whatever the math, this fact has no real effect on the significance of completing this magnificent run.

For many, that run ends below the Montenvers station where the adjacent Grand Hotel, built in 1870, is the first stop for a celebratory beer. From here, a short train ride returns you to Chamonix.

The Vallée Blanche has one last challenge, though, as you step off the ice—380 steps up a metal staircase to a short gondola that lifts you the final section up to the hotel and station; climbing the stairs after the long run is a final test of stamina.

Alternatively, if there's snow cover enough, you still have strength in your legs and you can wait a little longer for that beer, you can continue on—although there is an approximately 1,640-ft (500-m) stretch where skis must be removed; you then hike over glacial moraine before joining a snowy path down to Chamonix.

Whichever option you choose, you can enjoy the sense of personal achievement, not to mention relief, at having completed the world's longest lift-served ski run.

ABOVE: The Aiguille du Midi on the right, with its cable-car station perched precariously on top, and the mighty Mont Blanc behind—at 15,777ft (4,810m), the highest mountain in western Europe.

ABOVE: The first few turns when you set off from the saddle below the Aiguille are perilously steep and demand full commitment and concentration from the start.

Fact file La Vallée Blanche

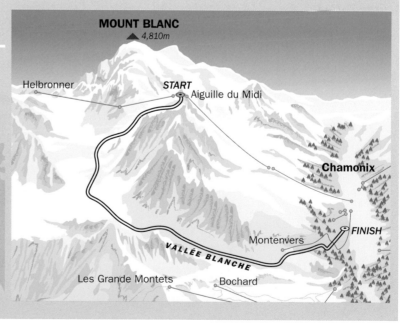

IN SHORT: The world's longest lift-served ski run

TOUGHNESS:
☠☠

FEAR FACTOR:
☠☠☠☠
(on the arête)

VERTICAL:
12,602–3,395ft
(3,842–1,035m)
(9,207ft/
2,807m vertical)

AVERAGE TIME:
Two hours

LENGTH OF RUN:
13.6 miles (22km)

ACCESS: Cable cars, then that arête to shuffle across

BEST TIME:
December–May

AVALANCHE KIT: Essential

ALTITUDE RANGE: 3,395–
12,602ft (1,035–3,842m)

SKIABLE AREA: 94. 2
miles (152km) (Mont Blanc
Unlimited pass:
496 miles/800km)

RUNS: 80

LIFTS: 47

WEB:
chamonix.com

GETTING THERE:
Geneva (54.5 miles/88km)

FRANCE

MOUNT BLANC
▲ 4,810m

Helbronner

START
Aiguille du Midi

Chamonix

Montenvers

FINISH

VALLÉE BLANCHE

Les Grande Montets

Bochard

Kandahar
Garmisch-Partenkirchen, Germany
5,576ft (1,700m)

The importance in skiing history of the Kandahar course at Garmisch-Partenkirchen cannot be overstated. The first Winter Olympic downhill ski races were staged upon it in 1936, and 75 years later the Alpine Skiing World Championships returned to its slopes for a second time. Numerous World Cup battles have also taken place here.

Garmisch is the undisputed winter-sports capital of Germany, located in its southeastern corner right on the Austrian border. Indeed, a lift ticket valid at several Austrian ski areas a few miles away is available, and in these days of the border-free European Union it can be hard to know you've "crossed over." It lies beneath the country's highest peak, the glacier-topped Zugspitz, also on that multiarea lift pass. But this is not the location of the Kandahar run, which instead is at one of the other medium-size ski areas surrounding the resort, currently named by marketeers as "Garmisch Classic," but traditionally named after the local ski hill, Kreuzeck.

What's in a name?

The name "Kandahar," also the second-largest city in Afghanistan, comes directly from British colonial and imperial power on a German ski run that was born just as the Nazi Party were rising to power. It has many interesting connotations in both the eternal battle to keep sport separate from politics, and the reality that many pioneers of skiing were either men of just such political power, or in danger of being influenced by them.

The shortest story of the unlikely connection of Kandahar with ski racing is tied to the pioneering British ski family, the Lunns (who founded the giant Lunn Poly travel agency, now absorbed into Thomson). They asked the famous British Field Marshall, Lord Roberts of Kandahar (who won decisive battles for the British in India and Afghanistan in the 19th century), to lend the status of his title to the first downhill ski races to be judged on speed, not style, that they were organizing, the earliest recorded at Crans Montana in 1911.

Arnold Lunn then fought for decades for ski racing to be added to

Host of the first Olympic downhill race nearly 80 years ago, Garmisch-Partenkirchen has played a key part in the development of downhill racing in Germany and around the world.

international snowsports competition. In the meantime, races and a famous ski club that still exists today were set up around Europe and further afield, all bearing the Kandahar name, even though Lord Roberts had died aged 82 in 1914 while inspecting Indian troops in France at the start of the First World War.

The first Winter Olympic downhill race

The Kandahar name's significance may be largely lost now, but the importance of Lord Roberts at the time cannot be overstated: he is one of the two nonroyals, the other being Winston Churchill, to lie in state in St. Pauls during the 20th century.

In the early 1930s Arnold Lunn was finally successful in achieving his dream, and the decision was finally taken to include downhill ski racing in the Winter Olympics. The Olympic course was designed and duly christened Kandahar. It was just a tad unfortunate that the Nazi Party had come to power shortly before the Games took place,

but perhaps a final victory for Lord Roberts. However, with skiing still generally the preserve of Europe's wealthy old guard, there was nothing like the Jesse Owens controversy at the summer Games in Berlin.

However controversial its roots (and perhaps they're something to ponder on as you whizz down it, along with the fact that it's so nice that we all get along these days), the Kandahar course has endured and is one of the oldest courses still hosting world-class competition. At the 2011 World Championships, super-G, giant slalom, and super combined events for men and women as well as the downhill were held on the Kandahar slope, which in the modern era has been divided into two parallel options, accessed by a modern, high-speed Kandahar-Express quad chairlift complete with heated seats for maximum comfort.

The Kandahar has many famous sections with suitably atmospheric names—Tröglhang, Heaven, Ice Slope, Hell—and it remains one of the most spectacular and technically demanding downhills of the World Cup circuit. The run (which is officially numbered number five on the piste map) was expanded for the 2011 Championships and the men now

race on a largely modified route, although the women's course follows much of the original Kandahar route. One of the most challenging sections of the men's slope now is the newly added Freefall section, which plummets at 92 percent, meaning taken at full speed the men's downhill now has four big jumps.

Together with the Middle Ski Path (number 13), accessed through a new ski tunnel, together with a third option, the upper part of the Olympia Run (number four), the three form the Kandahar Roundtrip, to make the most of your time on the slope.

Only a few other runs in the world have held races for so long and at all three top international levels, and no other can claim to be the first Olympic ski run; Kandahar is a must-ski.

ABOVE: A racer in the men's Alpine skiing World Cup event in Kandahar gets ready to follow in the tracks of history, along with sections temptingly named Hell and Ice Slope.

TOP RIGHT: This pretty forest scene belies the reality of a run with some of the steepest sections in downhill racing.

Fact file Kandahar

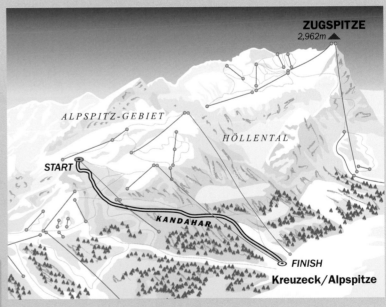

IN SHORT: The first Olympic downhill run, and still hosts the world's best nearly 80 years later

TOUGHNESS: ☠☠☠

FEAR FACTOR: ☠☠☠

VERTICAL: 5,576–2,821ft (1,700–860m) (3,083ft/940m vertical)

AVERAGE TIME: Two minutes (or more)

LENGTH OF RUN: 1.9 miles (3km)

ACCESS: Kreuzeck ski lift

BEST TIME: January–March

AVALANCHE KIT: Nonessential

ALTITUDE RANGE: 2,362–9,282ft (720–2,830m) (maximum vertical 4,428ft/1,350m)

SKIABLE AREA: 38.4 miles (62km)

RUNS: 34

LIFTS: 33

WEB: garmisch-partenkirchen.de zugspitze.de

GETTING THERE: Innsbruck (37.2 miles/60km), Munich (86.8 miles/140km)

GERMANY

ZUGSPITZE 2,962m ▲

ALPSPITZ-GEBIET

HÖLLENTAL

START

KANDAHAR

FINISH
Kreuzeck/Alpspitze

Dammkar
Mittenwald, Germany
7,360ft (2,244m)

LEFT: A short, roughly hewn tunnel connects the top station of the cable car with the top of the Dammkar. Take a moment to take in the view before you launch yourself into the void.

RIGHT: The top station of the Karwendelbahn has been in existence since 1966. The curious tube sitting next to it is the local nature information center with the fitting nickname *Fernrohr* (binocular), opened in 2008—a feat of modernist architecture.

Arguably Germany's most famous ski run, the Dammkar has been a "must ski" for every serious German skier for more than 80 years, and deserves to be more widely known.

It's a 4.7-mile- (7.5-km-) long off-piste descent through avalanche-prone terrain, initially taking you through classic high Alpine terrain with breathtaking panoramas, but then continuing down between mighty sheer rock walls as it continues its long descent.

The Dammkar run's colorful history dates back to the early years of downhill skiing in the 1930s, when hundreds of people would hike up the steep, 4,264 vertical feet (1,300m) from the exceptionally picturesque village of Mittenwald on any given day in order to ski down. The run was so popular that the sight of those hundreds of skiers ascending became known as the Dammkar worm until, in 1966, the Karwendelbahn cable car, which still operates today, was constructed. People hiked up no more, and the worm disappeared.

At that point the good people of Mittenwald (a village so pretty that, even back in the 18th century, it was described as "unspoilt by time") decided to try to create a modern ski resort, just as new ski areas were popping up all over the Alps. A groomer was procured that, attached to a winch, was able to smooth the once-unpisted slope, and Dammkar was promoted with the small nearby area of Kranzberg, which offers another 9.3 miles (15km) of ski runs. That *modus operandi* continued until the dawn of the modern freeriding era a decade ago, which happily coincided with the demise of the groomer, leaving the Dammkar once again in a natural state, and designated a "ski route."

Kaiserschmarrn mit Apfelmus

Skiing the Dammkar begins with the ten-minute ascent in the cable car to 7,360ft (2,244m), where breakfast in the restaurant awaits. The *Kaiserschmarrn mit Apfelmus und Preiselbeeren* (sugared pancake with raisins) is especially recommended (getting married there is also an option should the mood take you). From here there are views as far as the Zugspitz, but you may not wish to linger too long over food, views, or marriage that first time, especially if it's a fresh powder day.

Although the run begins some 5,248 vertical feet (1,600m) lower than the Vallée Blanche does, there is, or was, a similar issue in reaching the start of the descent—a tricky traverse above massive

Fact file Dammkar

IN SHORT: The worm may be dead but the run remains spectacular

TOUGHNESS:
☠☠☠☠☠

FEAR FACTOR:
☠☠☠

VERTICAL: 7,295–3,027ft (2,224–923m) (4,267ft/1,301m vertical)

AVERAGE TIME: One hour

LENGTH OF RUN: 4.7 miles (7.5km)

ACCESS: Dammkar cable car

BEST TIME: Jan–March

AVALANCHE KIT: Essential

ALTITUDE RANGE: 3,060–7,360ft (933–2,244m)

SKIABLE AREA: 18 miles (29km)

RUNS: 15

LIFTS: 8

WEB: karwendelbahn.de mittenwald.de

GETTING THERE: Innsbruck (18.6 miles/30km), Munich (85.6 miles/138km)

GERMANY

KARWENDELGEBIRGE
▲ 2,385m
START
Bergstation
DAMMKAR
KANONEN-ROHR
AM BANKERL
FINISH Talstation
Mittenwald

precipices on the face of the mountain dropping almost the full vertical, as did some unlucky skiers attempting that traverse 40 or more years ago.

The efficient German answer was, thankfully, to build a rough-hewn tunnel to the start of the run, which takes five minutes to tramp through. Even then, the beginning of the descent is slightly intimidating, with a ridge to ski that can be battered by strong winds and still has a fatal drop waiting for you if you take a wrong turn. It is best to take in that "top of the world" feeling and great views across the surrounding peaks before you start moving, then concentrate on your skiing.

You soon drop down onto more sheltered slopes, protected by spectacular sheer rock cliffs on each side. If the snow is fresh, you're likely to find the best powder of the entire run. Great vistas of the valley below appear as you descend toward the treeline and enter the latter stages of the run—essentially a path through the forest that ends right back at the cable-car base station, leaving you ready for your next lap.

A perfect Dammkar day

When to ski the Dammkar is a good question. The quality of the snow can vary tremendously, and while the odds of an enjoyable descent are typically at their greatest between January and March, a big fall of snow any time in winter or spring can leave the slopes in superb condition.

The lift company, however, in a dramatic failure to market the run by raising unrealistic expectations, is brutally honest: "Please note, there are only a few days in the winter where it is possible to have the perfect Dammkar day. We need a lot of snow to have perfect conditions. If you are one of these people who catch such an incredible ski day, you are amazingly lucky."

There are no official figures on "good days," but when pressed, the lift company estimates an average of perhaps 15 a season; sometimes more, sometimes less. This is because a poor winter can leave the slopes hard going for such a long descent, with stretches of icy moguls to contend with and possibly a walk of several miles at the bottom if the snowline has risen. Too much snow also means avalanche danger, especially if the warm *Föhn* wind, a feature of the area, blows in. Sometimes it's strong enough to stop the cable car.

However, the route is monitored by the Avalanche Commission and is only allowed to open once it's been declared safe and the weather is favorable. If this is the case, try to get to the lift (which runs every

half hour from 8.30 a.m.) early. A start between 9 a.m. and 11 a.m. is recommended. There's a Freeride Center at the Karwendelbahn base station where you can pick up tips for making the most of your day, as well as any equipment you need. There's also current information on the mountain's Facebook feed as well as on their own website.

But perhaps having a famous ski run that isn't great every day of the season—and sometimes not on any day all season—makes it all the more special, particularly if you happen to ski or board it on that rare perfect day and are, as the lift company says, "incredibly lucky."

With the addition of a rough-hewn tunnel to the start of the run, it is now a little easier to access the slope than it once was. You will still need a good head for heights, though, as the ridge has a fatal drop to one side if you take the wrong turn and is often battered by strong winds.

Valluga
Arlberg, Austria
9,220ft (2,811m)

The Arlberg has something of the mystical, something of the stuff of myth and legend for skiers. The ski area shared by half a dozen villages in the far west of Austria, most famously including Lech and St. Anton, has a reputation as home to some of the world's most challenging skiing, but equally as the "home" of downhill skiing. The Arlberg technique, one of the original styles of downhill skiing, was invented here.

The Arlberg today is one of the world's largest ski regions, too, expanding its extent to 211 miles (340km) of runs for the 2013–14 ski season when a lift connection was made to neighboring Warth and Schrocken from Lech.

But careful study of the piste map will reveal that these hundreds of miles of runs are not quite fully interconnected. There is a break with no lifts and no groomed ski runs between the highest lift-served point—the 9,220-ft- (2,811-m-) high Valluga peak—and the neighboring hamlet of Zürs, a village known for its five-star hotels and royal clientele. It is, however, possible to ski the connection, in one direction, so long as you are up to the challenge and in the company of an "Austrian certified guide."

RIGHT: Covering 210.8 miles (340km), the legend that is the Arlberg. **BELOW:** You need to be accompanied by a specially qualified guide to ski or board from the peak of Valluga, and when you do you'll have it all to yourself.

The Valluga runs are accessed by a series of decreasingly spacious cable cars from Galzig (7,167ft/2,185m) above St. Anton and St. Christoph. From here the Valluga I and II cable cars lift you to Vallugagrat (8,692ft/2,650m), the final point from which you can stop to eat in a restaurant or ski down a groomed run. You will only be allowed in the final Vallugabahn cable car to the top with ski gear if you are traveling with the aforementioned guide.

Peering over the edge

Once at that top station, one aspect that makes Valluga great, as with many of the runs in this book, is the view from the top, which is perched right on the very peak of the mountain. The 360-degree panorama from a specially constructed viewing platform here is truly spectacular, and most people arrive just to sightsee with many of the famous peaks of the eastern Alps visible. In fact, on a clear day you can see the mountains of five different countries—Austria, Italy, Switzerland, Liechtenstein, and Germany.

For those planning on skiing down, however, the immediate view is a little more intimidating as you peer nervously (and hopefully excitedly) over the edge. There are multiple routes down, with the starting points divided between the north and west sides (with pitches up to 40 degrees) or the still-more intimidating south side (with pitches of up to 50 degrees, meaning that it is less commonly skied).

The two most popular routes down the north and west faces both feed down into the Paziel valley, at the end of which a comfortable

LEFT: You should only attempt Valluga if you're an experienced off-piste skier or boarder and in the company of a guide, as the terrain is very steep and varied and finding your way if you're the first to break trail in fresh powder can be difficult.

six-seater chairlift, a very different experience to Vallugabahn II, takes you back up to the Zürs ski area.

For most on the classic north-face descent, it is the very first, serious, steep section of the run, lasting about 328ft (100m), that is the most unnerving, with the added intimidation of being watched from the terrace by curious onlookers. It is also potentially dangerous if you fall, which is more likely to happen earlier in the season if the slope is icy.

A fall could be potentially fatal, in fact, if you ski over the 656-ft (200-m) cliff, visible through a steep chute, on one edge, although the chances of that are unlikely unless you are seriously out of control—in which case you should not be there, and the guide you hired will have advised against doing the run.

This section is quite wide, so those who respect the challenge here and take their time should have no mishap of any degree and can complete it in three or four sweeping turns. Once this challenge has been mastered, the real pleasure of the descent is the vast, untracked powder fields that lie below, once out of view of the platform, in the long valley down to Zürs.

Transceiver, shovel, and probe

Valluga, like almost all off-piste skiing, is at its best with fresh snow cover. However, the combination of altitude, the limited number of skiers on the slopes, and the multiple route options does mean that the area cannot be "skied out" within hours of a storm, as it may be on other famous powder runs. Winter snow conditions are typically best on those north-facing slopes, but later in the season the long, south-facing runs below Erli Spitze often get nice, spring-like "firm" snow conditions.

As with any such steep, off-piste, high-mountain terrain, you need to be a relatively good skier, even with a guide. You should ideally have undergone at least some avalanche awareness training, and be equipped in case the worst should happen with transceiver, shovel, and probe.

Fact file Valluga

IN SHORT: Be one of the few to make the Arlberg connection

TOUGHNESS:
☠☠☠☠☠

FEAR FACTOR:
☠☠☠☠☠

VERTICAL: 9,220–5,642ft (2,811–1,720m) (3,578ft/1,091m vertical)

AVERAGE TIME: One hour

LENGTH OF RUN: 1.9 miles (3km)

ACCESS: Vallugabahn cable car

BEST TIME: Spring

AVALANCHE KIT: Essential

ALTITUDE RANGE: 4,277–9,220ft (1,304–2,811m)

SKIABLE AREA: 210.8 miles (340km)

RUNS: Not published

LIFTS: 94

WEB: stantonamarlberg.com

GETTING THERE: Innsbruck (64.5 miles/104km)

AUSTRIA

ARLBERG
START ▲ 2,811m

VALLUGA

FINISH

Zürs

St Christoph

Streif
Kitzbühel, Austria
6,560ft (2,000m)

Before you tackle this iconic run, it's important to stop and take in the scenic majesty all around you as well as the conditions of the slopes below. Maximum velocity can be reached very quickly on the iced run, which has sections with a gradient of 85 percent.

The Hahnenkamm, the most famous competition in the World Cup calendar and arguably the biggest annual sporting event in Austria, floods the famous resort of Kitzbühel with its fans on the last weekend of January each year. Actually the contest, with the big downhill race the main event on the Saturday, has expanded to fill most of the week, with more races including the World Cup Slalom and Giant Slalom on the preceding days and the Sunday.

Why so popular? Well the Hahnenkamm is, arguably again, the toughest race on the World Cup circuit, and getting down it in one piece, even better winning the race, takes exceptional guts as well as physical strength and technical ability. Racers touch 99.2 miles (160km) per hour on the fastest sections and plunge down gradients of up to 85 percent as they try to stay on their feet and maintain maximum velocity for 2 miles (3.3km).

The list of winners of the race is a *Who's Who* of the greats through the history of ski racing since the event was first staged in 1931. Toni Sailer won twice in the 1950s, while Jean-Claude Killy won in 1967, the year before sweeping the board at the Grenoble Winter Olympics, in 2:11.82 minutes, a record speed that stood for seven years. Franz Klammer won three times in the 1970s, before sensationally retaking the title nearly ten years after his first win, in 1984. Before Klammer's fourth win, during a high in Canadian ski racing talent, three Canadian racers and fellow Canadian Ken Read had won four of the five previous races; and in 1987 the great Swiss racer, Pirmin Zurbriggen, became the first to complete the course in under two minutes with a time of 1:58.06. In 2012 Didier Cuche, another great Swiss racer, became the first man to win the race five times, but the current record (at the time of writing) descent speed of 1:51.58 was set back in 1997 by the Austrian, Fritz Strobl.

A catapult start

There is, in fact, no run called the Hahnenkamm; the race takes place on the Streif piste but the good news is that you do not need to be a World Cup racer to try it, although you might wish you were. Arrive in the resort the week after the Hahnenkamm has taken place and you have the chance to ski the race course yourself, conditions permitting and with the permission of the resort if you're planning to tackle it at high speed. You'll also need race-prepared skis in order to have a chance of getting a grip on the icy surface.

If you do ski the course with permission and a guide in the days after the race, you'll be able to get the full experience—assuming you can stay on your feet. Many who try fall at the very first hurdle, the very steep start that catapults racers toward maximum velocity very quickly on the iced run.

Survive that and the most alarming section is up next with an 85 percent gradient, a whole seven percent more than Austria's steepest regular groomed run, Harakiri at Mayrhofen, which you won't hit at full speed anyway. The course then drops into the Mausfalle (the "Mousetrap"). Racers hit it at around 93 miles (150km) per hour, typically leaping around 262ft (80m) through the air, not a lot short of a conventional ski jump. If you don't land properly back on your feet here, a long, very fast slide will be the result, with a strong chance of a hospital visit soon after.

LEFT: Race day at the Hahnenkamm, one of the world's great sporting events—and one of ski racing's most iconic and historic—staged for more than 80 years and regarded by some Alpine racers as more important to win than a Winter Olympic gold.

However, despite the challenges of the vertical, most racers feel that it is not the steep and airborne stretches that are the problem, but the Steilhang that comes next. This features a reverse camber, which essentially means that, as you try to turn, the slope falls away beneath you. Get any of these sections wrong when the time counts and you'll be punished by losing speed coming into some of the long, flatter sections that follow, making up the lower two-thirds of the course.

After the respite of the gliding section, the beginning of the end comes at the Hausbergkante jump, then across the Querfahrt before the Zielschuss finishing straight, where World Cup racers reach maximum speeds of 86.8 miles (140km) per hour. One last jump and you cross the finishing line at Rasmusleiten right above Kitzbühel where, in your imagination, tens of thousands of wildly cheering fans are screaming you in.

Relive the Hahnenkamm

Even without special permission and a guide to oversee you, you can ski the route of the Hahnenkamm at most other times of the season, when no competitive races are being held, though it is usually closed for preparation throughout January. The trail does change, however, and it is then classified as an off-piste route. This essentially means that it isn't groomed, so the steepest sections often become steep mogul fields, which of course present considerable challenges in themselves. The flatter parts are absorbed into gentler, groomed pistes, which are easier to ski but shouldn't be tackled at full speed owing to beginners and intermediates carving their way at a leisurely pace along them. You can also relive all the great moments of the race over its more than 80-year history at the Hahnenkamm lift's top station, where a race museum is open from 9 a.m. to 4 p.m. daily and is free to visit.

So will you be the next Klammer, Killy, or Cuche? No. But staying on your feet to the end of the Hahnenkamm is success enough for most.

Fact file Streif

IN SHORT: The greatest high-speed challenge if you're not in a machine

TOUGHNESS:
(if taken at full speed)

FEAR FACTOR:
(if taken at full speed)

VERTICAL: 5,461–2,640ft (1,665–805m) (2,821ft/860m vertical)

AVERAGE TIME: 2 mins

LENGTH OF RUN: 2 miles (3.312km)

ACCESS: Hahnenkammbahn lift

BEST TIME: The week after the final weekend in January

AVALANCHE KIT: Nonessential

ALTITUDE RANGE: 2,624–6,560ft (800–2,000m)

SKIABLE AREA: 104.2 miles (168km)

RUNS: 60

LIFTS: 52

WEB: hahnenkamm.com bergbahn-kitzbuehel.at kitzbuehel.com kitzalps.com

GETTING THERE: Salzburg (49.6 miles/80km), Innsbruck (56 miles/90km)

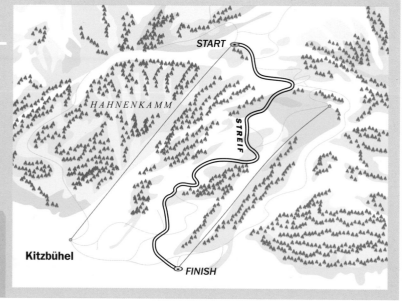

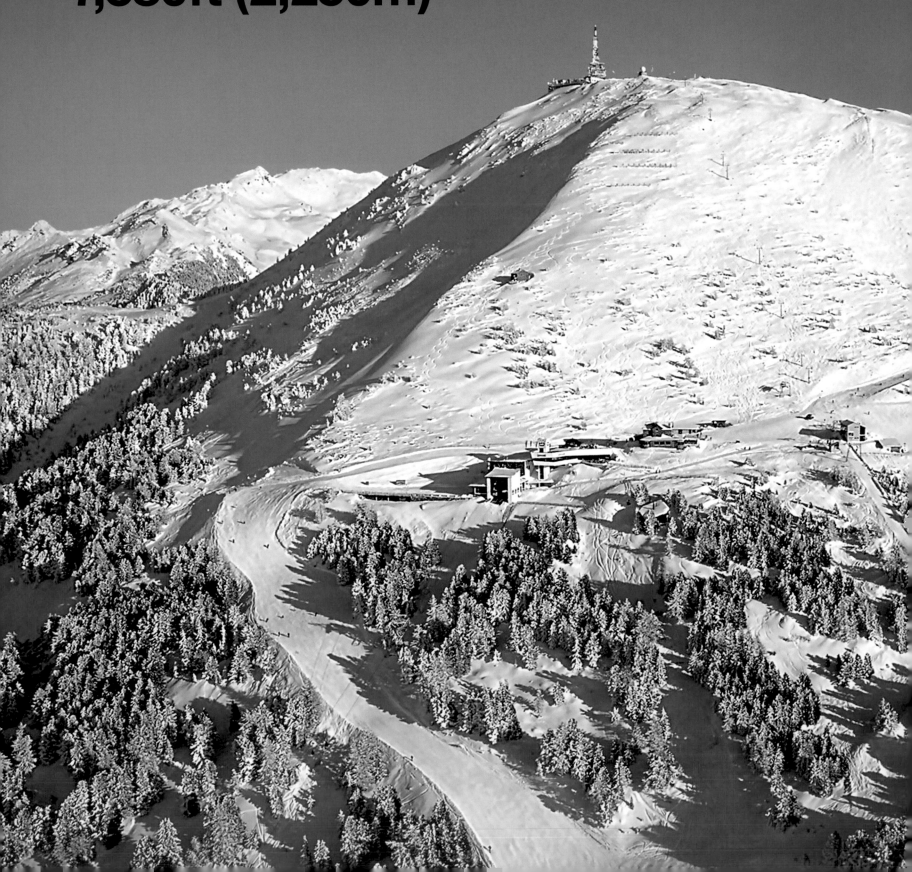

Olympia Run
Patscherkofel, Austria
7,380ft (2,250m)

There's only one ski run in the world that can claim to have hosted the blue-ribbon ski-racing events at three separate Olympic Games.

To those not well versed in Winter Olympic history, the little village of Igls, perched above the city of Innsbruck, the capital of Austria's world-famous Tirol region, is not a well-known ski resort either. Yet with its unassuming 12.4 miles (20km) of largely family-friendly, easy-, and intermediate-standard skiing, it does indeed hold that unique distinction.

And the Olympics it has hosted are not just any old Games, either. The first time, in 1964, the race was won by Austrian Egon Zimmermann, but when the Games returned just 12 years later in 1976 (when eventual 2010 Games' hosts Whistler rejected an IOC offer to stage them), the Patscherkofel witnessed what is still one of the greatest Olympic downhill races ever, when a young Franz Klammer, then aged 22, edged out the Swiss racer Bernhard Russi by 0.33 seconds to take gold.

Klammer was traveling at an average speed of 63.7 miles (102.8km) per hour on the 10-ft- (3-km-) long course to take his win in 1:45.73 minutes.

Russi, who had won gold in the downhill at the previous 1972 Winter Olympics in Sapporo, Japan, as well as enjoying several other major career wins, went on to design many of the Olympic downhill ski runs of later games, including those for Albertville (1992), Lillehammer (1994), and Nagano (1998) among others. More recently, he also designed the Grizzly run at Snowbasin for the 2002 Salt Lake Games and the Sochi downhill course from the most recent Olympics, both included in this book.

The ultimate groomed run

What makes the Olympia run, graded a red, so special? It's beautifully groomed and can happily be taken at a steady pace by a competent intermediate skier, but so are thousands of other runs around the world—so why the reputation?

For many, this is the perfect groomed ski run. Of all the runs in all the world with all their different lengths, pitches, terrain, orientation, fall lines, and 101 other variable factors, the Olympia run gets it dead

BELOW: Igls is a family-friendly resort that remains relatively undiscovered by those not well versed in Winter Olympic history. With the city of Innsbruck spread out below, it is unassuming and contains many easily accessible runs for those with a basic level of skiing ability.

120 | **Olympia Run, Patscherkofel**

right, with near-perfect scores for every individual factor that can make a groomed run great and satisfying in every way.

For good skiers to really enjoy the Olympia Run as they should, it means seeing if you can come close to Klammer's speed of over 62 miles (100km) per hour, and that means signing up for racing classes. Indeed, race training is a big part of the Patscherkofel operation, with two permanent race-training runs (separate to Olympia), floodlit skiing, and Wednesday night being reserved for racing only. The run is also sometimes open, freshly groomed and in pristine condition, from 7.30–9.30 a.m. for racers only. The center capitalizes on its reputation and easy-to-reach location, with air, rail, and highway links straight to Innsbruck and then a fast funicular up to the slopes; a cable car takes you on, straight to the top of the mountain.

A high-speed cruise

The Olympia descent is just over 10ft (3km) long and descends on a curving, technical course through the forest, but you can begin from the top of the ski area, above the treeline, for the full 4,428-ft (1,350-m)

vertical and a 3.2-mile- (5.1-km-) long, high-speed cruise. Many people do laps on this course.

And finally ... the Olympic bobsleigh run

And let's not forget the other pleasures of Patscherkofel, even for nonracers. The slopes afford wonderful views out over Innsbruck, the capital of the Tirol, a spectacular sight as you descend. All around the city are dotted more ski areas, and the Olympic Ski Pass gives access both to the runs of all eight of them (most visible across the city as you ski down Olympia) and public transport in between them, located as they are 15–60 minutes away from Igls, and including the snowsure Stubai glacier.

If you don't manage to break the 62-mile- (100-km)-per-hour mark on the Olympia run, you can always do so, guaranteed, on Igls' other Olympic legacy feature—its bobsleigh run. Here you ride in a "taxi bob" behind a professional driver and in front of a professional brake-man, and reach up to 71.3 miles (115km) per hour as you hurtle down the track, hitting up to two g-force.

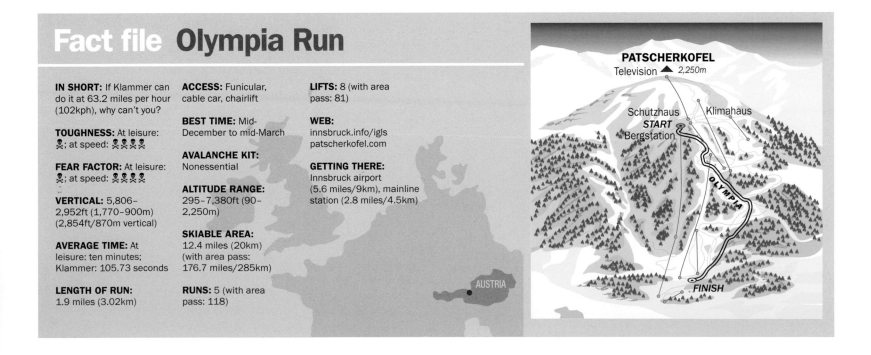

Fact file Olympia Run

IN SHORT: If Klammer can do it at 63.2 miles per hour (102kph), why can't you?

TOUGHNESS: At leisure: ☠; at speed: ☠☠☠☠

FEAR FACTOR: At leisure: ☠; at speed: ☠☠☠☠

VERTICAL: 5,806–2,952ft (1,770–900m) (2,854ft/870m vertical)

AVERAGE TIME: At leisure: ten minutes; Klammer: 105.73 seconds

LENGTH OF RUN: 1.9 miles (3.02km)

ACCESS: Funicular, cable car, chairlift

BEST TIME: Mid-December to mid-March

AVALANCHE KIT: Nonessential

ALTITUDE RANGE: 295–7,380ft (90–2,250m)

SKIABLE AREA: 12.4 miles (20km) (with area pass: 176.7 miles/285km)

RUNS: 5 (with area pass: 118)

LIFTS: 8 (with area pass: 81)

WEB: innsbruck.info/igls patscherkofel.com

GETTING THERE: Innsbruck airport (5.6 miles/9km), mainline station (2.8 miles/4.5km)

PATSCHERKOFEL
Television ▲ 2,250m

Schutzhaus   Klimahaus
START
Bergstation

AUSTRIA

OLYMPIA

FINISH

Edelgriess
Dachstein, Austria
8,856ft (2,700m)

With access via a tunnel, ladder, and traversing a "no falling zone," the start of the famous Edelgriess run may be a bit of a hike to get to, but what a hike, and what a reward!

Although it's fair to say that Austria is not as well known for high-mountain terrain as perhaps France or Switzerland, with many of the best-known ski areas peaking below 6,560ft (2,000m), there are, nonetheless, plenty of exceptions. They are made possible by the snow-rich Austrian winters and countless great north-facing slopes.

The planet's greatest lift-served verticals

But if you combine uncharacteristically high Austrian peaks (one of those exceptions ...) with typically low Austrian valleys and throw in a healthy snowfall, you have the potential for some of the longest ski runs on the planet over the greatest lift-served verticals.

One of those Austrian high points is in the southern province of Styria. The Dachstein glacier, a year-round snowsports haven, peaks at just below 8,856ft (2,700m) above sea level. It is located close to the famous resort of Schladming, a multiple host to the Alpine Skiing World Championships (most recently in 2013), and can claim to be a long-time favorite of actor and former Californian governor Arnold Schwarzenegger, as well as where the great skier Franz Klammer notched up his first win. Villages below the glacier sit as low as 1,676ft (511m) above sea level, leaving the potential of nearly 7,216-ft (2,200-m) lift-served descents—in other words, some of the longest possible on earth.

Fairly challenging to extreme

There are no marked and groomed pistes down, and for most runs there is no direct lift back up, but the top of the run can be reached by cable car, and a return trip to the bottom of that cable car once you finish your run is quite simple by bus.

BELOW: From the top of Edelgriess, take a moment to breathe in the scenery of snowy peaks stretching toward Slovenia and Italy. And now switch to matters closer at hand, like the intimidating drop down to the Dachstein glacier that you've committed yourself to tackle.

Choosing your route is a tough choice, with eight major options ranging in difficulty from fairly challenging to extreme. The 15.5-mile- (25-km-) long Austrian National ski tour, which crosses the glacier and descends 7,177 vertical feet (2,188m) to the lakeside village of Hallstadt, is here, and the options include the challenging Schwadering, a 3,280-ft (1,000-m) vertical descent that takes you back to the cable-car base station. There is also the Fluder, a very steep and extremely long descent between the limestone walls of the Scheichenspitze down to Ramsau, which is regarded as the most challenging.

However, I've opted here for the Edelgriess run, an 11.2 mile- (18-km) downhill route that crosses the Dachstein massif down to Ramsau over 5,248 vertical feet (1,600m). The local ski school rates this as "moderate" compared to the aforementioned options, but with pitches of up to 50 degrees in places, and access via a tunnel, ladder, and traversing a "no falling zone," actually getting to the top of the run involves overcoming a considerable fear factor. To add to the fun, or the fear, the cable car that accesses Edelgriess and the rest of the Dachstein glacier's numerous attractions recently had a multimillion euro overhaul, with the new-look lift unveiled in the summer of 2013 with a novel new attraction— the option to ride up outdoors on a "balcony" added to the roof of the lift for the 3,280-ft (1,000-m) vertical ascent. It's first come, first served at the base station to get into this rooftop terrace with a difference.

Access via tunnel and rockface

Once at the top station, there's a short ski and a short draglift ride (lift E on the map) to where the experience proper begins, if not the run. You climb three difficult medal ladders in succession, a total ascent of some 66ft (20m), in the cliff face, wearing your ski boots, of course, with your skis strapped to your backpack (this can be one of those times when being a boarder is better), then pass through the rough-hewn Koppen Stollen tunnel that takes you from the north to the south side of the rock face (there are doors on it to stop too much snow blowing in).

Once out on the south side, take a breath and enjoy the phenomenal views out over the mountains of the Lower Tauerm—it's that "top of the world" feeling. Next comes the traverse, with some safety ropes, before you reach, at last, the top of the Edelgriess run, which is located on the west side of a ridge.

One regular on the route summed up the overall experience: "It always makes you realize that death is never too far off, which I think is a good feeling." The first part of the descent crosses magnificent wide-open powder fields as you ski through the wide, 0.62-mile- (1-km-) long corrie between the Türlspitz and Gamsfeldspitz, with their rocky walls towering above. If conditions are right this will be perfect powder, perfectly pitched and really one of those "It doesn't get better than this!" moments.

The descent is broken by a short traverse into the Kramllahn before arriving above Ramsau for the lower half of the descent over another 1,640 vertical feet (500m) down to the village. The slope has an eastern exposure first, then later a generally southern orientation. Avalanches and rock falls are a regular problem and the run is only open when considered relatively safe (those tunnel doors are closed when dangerous). It is therefore still vital to opt for a certified guide, as well as carrying your avalanche safety equipment and knowing how to use it.

ABOVE: Spectacular skiing meets spectacularly scary traverse before you set off on the 3.72-mile- (6-km-) long, off-piste Edelgriess descent.

Fact file Edelgriess

IN SHORT:
Hang hundreds of feet in the air, climb a ladder, go through a tunnel, along a ridge, and then you can start!

TOUGHNESS:
☠☠☠

FEAR FACTOR:
☠☠☠

VERTICAL: 8,856–3,608ft (2,700–1,100m)

AVERAGE TIME:
90 minutes

LENGTH OF RUN:
3.72 miles (6km)

ACCESS: Cable car, draglift, ladder, cave, traverse

BEST TIME: February–March

AVALANCHE KIT:
Essential

ALTITUDE RANGE:
2,444–8,856ft (745–2,700m)

SKIABLE AREA:
138.3 miles (223km)

RUNS: 54

LIFTS: 14

WEB:
schladming-dachstein.at
skischule-ramsau.at

GETTING THERE:
Salzburg (49.6 miles/80km)

AUSTRIA

DACHSTEIN ▲ 2,700m
Sky Walk
START
Talstation
EDELGRIESS
SCHEICHENSPITZE
Ramsau **FINISH**

Wilde Grub'n
Stubai, Austria
10,529ft (3,210m)

Some 6.2 miles (10km) long with up to 4,953ft (1,510m)
of vertical, Austria's famous Wilde Grub'n ski route is
eternally popular and exceptionally good whenever fresh
powder has fallen. The pleasure just goes on and on.

> **" YOU'LL SEE A VAST BOWL BELOW, WITH SKIERS' TRACKS BOUNCING AROUND LIKE THE HIGHWAYS IN A ROADRUNNER CARTOON. "**

Fact file **Wilde Grub'n**

IN SHORT: Ride this twisting and varied 6.2 mile (10km) off-piste route winding through a dramatic open bowl and finishing at the base station

TOUGHNESS:
☠☠

FEAR FACTOR:
☠☠

VERTICAL: 10,529–5,740ft (3,210–1,750m) (4,789ft/1,460m vertical)

AVERAGE TIME:
30 minutes

LENGTH OF RUN:
6.2 miles (10km)

ACCESS: Cable car, drag and chairlifts

BEST TIME: January–April

AVALANCHE KIT:
Essential

ALTITUDE RANGE: 5,740–10,529ft (1,750–3,210m)

SKIABLE AREA:
38.4 miles (62km)

RUNS: 35

LIFTS: 26

WEB:
stubaier-gletscher.com
freeridecenter-stubai.com

GETTING THERE:
Innsbruck (24.8 miles/40km)

AUSTRIA

STUBAIER WILDSPITZE
3,340m ▲

START

Mittelstation Fernau

WILDE GRUB'N

Talstation

FINISH

Although it's a well-used route and only open when safe, riders can make use of the Stubai's Freeride Checkpoints at the bottom station of Mutterberg or the downloadable app, which provides up-to-date information on avalanche conditions.

When does an officially designated off-piste ski route become so popular that it requires top-to-bottom snowmaking? When it's the Wilde Grub'n run, officially ski route 14 on the piste map, which descends for a remarkable 6.2 miles (10km) over 4,789ft (1,460m) of vertical from the top of the Stubai glacier, one of Austria's highest lift-served points at 10,529ft (3,210m) and a ski area normally open for nine months of the year.

The question of whether Wilde Grub'n is one of the world's best runs will be one that taxes the minds of those who love their slopes to be steep and deep in powder, as it isn't the former and rarely the latter of those two things. What it is, is very long, one of Austria's longest descents in fact, and great fun as it bounces around the glacial moraine on its long way down to the valley. So it's included in this book for that often forgotten virtue of the great run—the simple, pure, enduring pleasure of a fast, fun ski run.

The challenge and gradient of the trail varies between a blue and a red grade (although you can mix in some black above) and it's easy to pick up speed on the upper sections of the wide-open glacier before the more challenging ski route number 14 begins below.

Adding in a glacier black run

There are multiple routes across the ski slopes before you reach the top of Wilde Grub'n itself, including taking the newly installed Daunjoch quad chairlift up to 9,840ft (3,000m) above sea level and beginning your run on the new black slope, Daunhill (number 22)—the steepest slope in the area with a maximum pitch of 31 degrees—then switching onto Wilde Grub'n where it begins at 10,529ft (3,210m) up. This shortens the length of your overall descent and cuts the vertical to 4,067ft (1,240m), but does add the challenge of a mile-long glacier black run to the top.

For the full run, however, it's the classic descent down from 10,529ft (3,210m) above sea level on blue run number seven, known as Daufenerer. This is a classic fast, wide, more than 1.9-mile- (3-km-) long glacier blue run. You take a turn to skier's right off onto another blue, 23, three-quarters of the way down, in order to reach the top of Wilde Grub'n at Gamsgarten.

Once you're on Wilde Grub'n itself, you'll see an expanse of whiteness stretched out across a vast bowl below you, with skiers' tracks (unless you're lucky enough to be there first) bouncing around like the highways in a Roadrunner cartoon. The route takes you far off to skier's left of the main lifts back up on the glacier above, so, depending on how busy the run is as you make your descent, you can feel a million miles from the rest of the world at times.

The Powder Department

Whichever route you take from the top, once you've skied it (and it's best to do it early, as it gets busy later in the day as everyone heads down it to avoid needing to take the lift back down), you can if you wish seek out greater challenges on the Stubai.

The resort has been bolstering its appeal to freeriders in recent seasons with ever-faster, more comfortable lifts to get to the top of the slopes, but also some of the best facilities for freeriders to be found anywhere.

The resort's "Powder Department" is a one-stop store in which you can sign up for classes, hire a guide, test your avalanche safety equipment and your knowledge of how to use it, and get the latest information on conditions. There's also an app that provides live information on 15 of the most popular freeride routes on the mountain, which have catchy names such as Cannonball, Thriller Flake, The Wall, and North Face. Use the app's geo-location device and it will tell you where you are on the run, or indeed if you have left the run altogether. It also provides live weather information and details of the current avalanche conditions.

Whether or not you download the app, you can make use of the Stubai's Freeride Checkpoints at the bottom station of Mutterberg and at Eisgrat where similar information is provided, and at Gamsgarten there are regular avalanche safety training sessions. The region also has many more serious ski tours to undertake with a guide, and there's even a Freeride lounge down in the valley at Neustift where you can arrange tours and gather the latest information, too.

So whether you take the long, fun Wilde Grub'n or something steeper and more strenuous, you can always enjoy the big verticals, great views, and very professional organization of the Stubai.

Wilde Grub'n has its steep stretches, its smoother, faster sections, and its enduring length, but whichever part you enjoy the most, that pleasure is magnified on a perfect powder day with blue sky above.

Inferno
Mürren, Switzerland
9,742ft (2,970m)

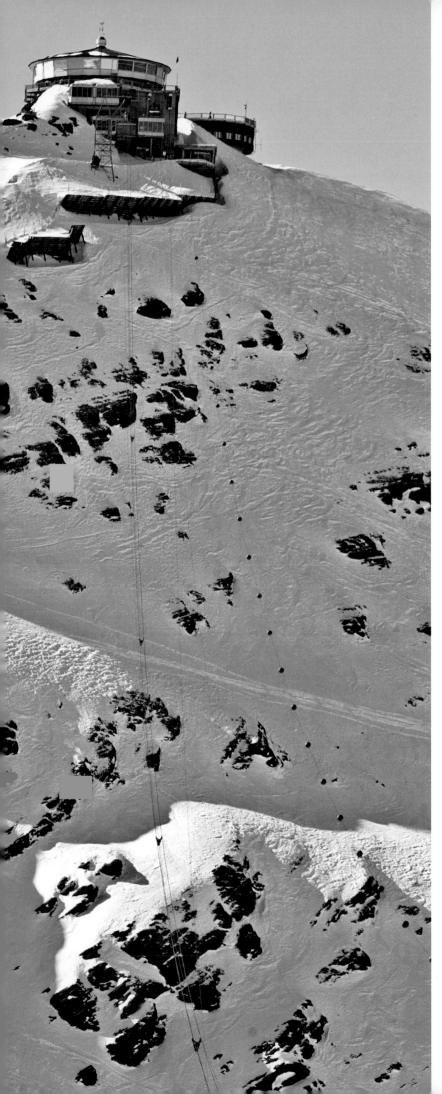

The Inferno is both a ski race and a ski run. The run does not really officially exist, except when the race is being staged, although if conditions are good you may be able to recreate it. That would be in the spirit of the thing because, when the great British ski-racing pioneer Sir Arnold Lunn (see also the Kandahar run at Garmisch-Partenkirchen on pages 102–105) stood at the top of the course to compete with 16 others from the Kandahar Ski Club in that first race on a crisp, clear morning on January 29, 1928, the run didn't officially exist then, either.

That first race was won by Harold Mitchell in a time of one hour, 12 minutes, and all 17 competitors completed the descent. Three years later Lunn had finally won official recognition of Alpine ski racing as a World Cup sport and staged the first Alpine Skiing World Championships at Mürren, the next step on the way to having it adopted as a Winter Olympic discipline (the early Games did not feature downhill skiing).

The lineup

More than 85 years later and with the race having been staged in late January more than 70 times (only eight were staged between 1930 and 1950, but after that it ran almost every other year), the competition is now the world's biggest downhill ski event. It is the biggest both in terms of the vertical (6,527ft/1,990m of it) and also the number of participants—limited to around 1,800, but usually oversubscribed at least twice over each year. Open to all, amateurs and professionals alike, it's important to subscribe early if you want to have a chance of getting a starting bib. The race opens for entries the August prior to race day and is invariably full within a week.

The pretty, car-free, and historic resort of Mürren itself is little changed over those eight-and-a-half decades. Still home to a few hundred farmers, it has resisted the expansion of many other famous Swiss ski areas and instead retains all of its traditional charm, as well as jaw-dropping scenery that's more or less unmatched anywhere in the skiing world.

LEFT: Piz Gloria, the famous revolving restaurant above Mürren and the start of the Inferno race course, offers spectacular views of the stunning Jungfrau region's scenery all around.

On Her Majesty's Secret Service

You don't need to ski up to the top of the course on the Schilthorn from Mürren, as Sir Arnold and other members of the Kandahar Ski Club had to. Today it's a cable-car ride up to the revolving Piz Gloria restaurant, nearly 9,840ft (3,000m) up, before skiing down to the start of the course at 9,151ft (2,790m).

But unless you're late to get to your starting slot (and you don't want to miss it, as skiers depart every few seconds), it's worth spending a while at that restaurant, taking in some of the most spectacular scenery in the world—with the Eiger, Monch, and Jungfrau peaks ahead of you. You can also gain inspiration from the James Bond exhibition and themed meals served here, as this was where Mr. Bond battled baddies in the 1970 movie *On Her Majesty's Secret Service*, and the resulting income from the movie company helped fund its completion.

The annual starting lineup of the Inferno sees competitors from at least 20 nations as well as members of the Kandahar Ski Club competing together. There's normally a Lunn there, too, with Arnold's son Peter racing into his 90s and now grandson Stephen taking up the family mantle.

ABOVE: Outside of race day, much of the route of the Inferno can be enjoyed like a regular slope, snow cover permitting.

Racers depart the starting gate every 12 seconds for more than six-and-a-half hours after the first racer at 8.50 a.m. Usually the best, clad in catsuits and on 1.4-mile- (2.2-m-) long racing skis, go first. Even without better technique and stamina, wearing that racing equipment is likely to give at least a two-minute advantage over the later entrants, who are more likely to be clad in regular recreational gear and taking the race aspect of the Inferno less seriously. That's a good job, as they'll have to battle through the ruts created by the hundreds that have gone before. A competent skier will complete the 10.4-mile (16.8-km) course in around 45 minutes, while the fastest complete it in less than 15 minutes. Indeed, they keep getting faster: the record was broken again in 2013, taking the fastest descent time down to just over 13 minutes, 20 seconds—cutting almost an hour off that 1928 winning time.

RIGHT: There's more to the Inferno weekend than "just" the race itself—there's also the ceremonial burning of a devil effigy; an offering to the ski-racing gods. The ritual is thought to bring the racers good luck.

FAR RIGHT: Inaugurated by Sir Arnold Lunn of Britain, widely considered the father of Alpine ski racing and responsible for introducing slalom and downhill to the Olympics in 1936, signs go up for the Inferno race every January.

The run itself, more than 9.9 miles (16km) long, crosses the Engetal to the Schilthorn Hut before moving into a long S-shaped route below the Muttlerenhorn.

Next comes the challenging Kanonenrohr before a "double S" followed by a sharp right curve. This upper section of the course requires strong thigh muscles to make the turns, and to carry speed competitors need to find the optimal line through the S-bends.

Then it's a case of mastering the best gliding technique as the route enters woodland, crossing the path of the Maulerhubel lift before a slight ascent leads to Winteregg and over the Winteregg Bridge, joining the forest track down toward Lauterbrunnen. In some sections a skating step is required to maintain momentum as well as using your arms. And however fit you are (and you do need to be as fit as you can), mental strength can be the crucial factor if you want to maintain your technique all the way down and post a respectable time.

Overall, the Inferno race challenges all aspects of your skiing and is therefore best suited to the "all-rounder." The official documentation explains: "The upper part of the course demands downhill turning technique and an optimal line. The middle section calls for an ideal downhill position and fast gliding. From the Kanonenrohr to the Höhenlücke, technically superior skiers come into their own. Over the stretch from Maulerhubel to Winteregg, skating step and arm power can be all-important. And from Winteregg–Spriessenkehr to Lauterbrunnen, optimal equipment, a clean downhill position and—not least—mental stamina can be the key to a fast final time."

If getting into the race is a challenge in itself for most, then making the full vertical all the way down to Lauterbrunnen in the valley is an added one. On average, conditions are only good enough these days one season in every decade for that full vertical to be possible. Most years it has to be shortened to wherever the snowline is.

But wherever it ends, there's a party to be had once you and all the other competitors have finished the race. Back up in Mürren there is dancing and entertainment, along with the prize-giving, which continue until 3 a.m. on the Sunday morning if you have the stamina to carry on through.

In any case, if you're lucky enough to get in the race, and even more lucky to be able to make the full vertical, it's an experience you'll never forget for your whole skiing life.

Fact file Inferno

IN SHORT: The greatest ski race on earth

TOUGHNESS:
☠☠☠

FEAR FACTOR:
☠☠☠

VERTICAL: 9,742–2,624ft (2,970–800m) (7,118ft/2,170m vertical, including the run down to the start)

AVERAGE TIME: 15–45 minutes

LENGTH OF RUN: 10.4 miles (16.8km)

ACCESS: Cable car

BEST TIME: Late January

AVALANCHE KIT: Nonessential

ALTITUDE RANGE: 2,624–9,742ft (800–2,970m)

SKIABLE AREA: 132 miles (213km)

RUNS: 81

LIFTS: 44

WEB: inferno-muerren.ch kandahar.org.uk jungfrauwinter.ch

GETTING THERE: Zurich (93 miles/150km)

SWITZERLAND

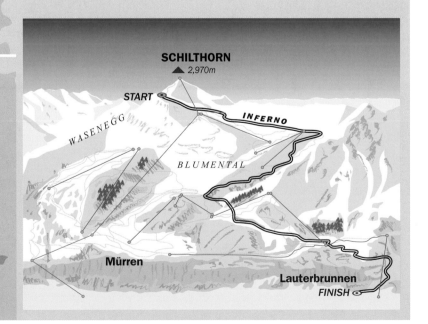

SCHILTHORN
▲ 2,970m

START

INFERNO

WASENEGG

BLUMENTAL

Mürren

Lauterbrunnen
FINISH

Backside
Verbier, Switzerland
10,824ft (3,300m)

Verbier's sterling reputation among the world's best skiers is well deserved. Indeed, rather like Chamonix and St. Anton, the abundance of great ski terrain for advanced and expert skiers and a corresponding lack of abundant easy and intermediate-level stuff (although there's plenty of it) can come as a shock to those not really capable of enjoying the tough stuff but lured by the big name.

The fact that there are, officially, few black-graded runs here adds to the confusion. That's partly because many former black runs have been reclassified as "off-piste routes" (there are more than 74.4 miles/120km of them), with a different legal status and maintenance requirements.

Modern living

Verbier is, in fact, one of the more modern and created communities in Swiss skiing. Like many of the famous French ski villages just over the border, 60 years ago there was very little here except pasture land and a few cow sheds. It did not have the climbing history of Chamonix or the Grand Tour history of St. Moritz. Instead, resort designers had a blank canvas and their design has been such a success that the resort now sits at the heart of one of Switzerland's largest lift-linked ski systems, the Four Valleys.

But although it may be considered one of the new arrivals in the long history of Swiss winter-sports vacations, which now stretches back 150 years, Verbier has certainly made its mark, with events such as the freeriding and speed-skiing world tours all ending up here each spring. For expert skiers, the options in Verbier are relatively limitless and agreeing the best run at this one resort is a kind of microcosm of agreeing the best runs on the entire planet—everyone has their own, strong opinion.

Many fans of Verbier opt for the Chaussoure run on Tortin, a very steep, often icy descent (but glorious in powder conditions), famed for growing giant moguls by midwinter and for being accessed via a fairly alarming traverse.

The ultimate off-piste classic

However, the "Backside" of Mont Fort, as the local freeriding community refer to it, is generally agreed by tourists and locals alike to be *the* classic, off-piste run in Verbier and a worthy entry on the international powder hunter's must-do list. Why? Its ease of access, long vertical drop of 5,248ft (1,600m), and the chance to make multiple variants on the routes make it the best run in the valley.

After a snowstorm there will frequently be twice as much snow in the upper couloirs as on any of the other descents in Verbier. But if you're not a highly skilled local, you need to hire a guide to ski it. Indeed, local guides are often hired JUST to do it.

The payback for your pleasure

To access the run, start by riding the Mont Fort cable car to the top and walk down the stairs. Then, instead of skiing down the face under the lift, go left under the rope leading to the backside of the mountain.

The first traverse here is critical. If there is any avalanche danger, the risk of getting caught in a slide 1,968ft (600m) down the south face is not pretty. After this hair-raising short traverse of 262ft (80m), one arrives on the backside with its north-facing couloirs. The first one you get to is a beautiful gully to open slopes, which then leads into another narrow chute. From here, the run becomes a long and winding ride to the Cleuson lake, with several bowls and slopes to ski *en route*.

Once you reach the lake it is payback time for your pleasure, with a traverse along the lake's flat right bank for a 0.62 mile (1km). Remember: no pain, no gain! So here you will need to impress with your double fall-line skating technique to avoid the embarrassment of being passed by everyone else on the mountain. If you're on a board, take it off and hike. Once you reach the dam, stop and rest, and enjoy the sight of the others suffering in your tracks.

After your break, it's time to descend once more and drop straight down beside the dam. If there's fresh power and you still have the legs, you can enjoy the novelty of making a few inverted turns off the snow- and ice-coated concrete dam, but be careful not to edge too hard to avoid rounding your edges.

At the bottom of the dam you'll reach a road that rejoins the pistes to Siviez, from where you can take the lift back to Tortin.

Getting first tracks down this steep line after a big dump is indeed the ultimate Verbier experience, which the locals aim for while the tourists battle it out on better-known runs. The winner gets not only a run they'll remember for years but also first-tracks bragging rights for their feat, at the Pub Mont Fort that night.

Be prepared for some steep terrain on Verbier's Backside – especially at the top as you drop into a sudden narrow chute.

Fact file Backside

IN SHORT: The toughest run at the toughest resort

TOUGHNESS:
☠☠☠☠☠

FEAR FACTOR:
☠☠☠☠☠

VERTICAL: 10,922–5,674ft (3,330m–1,730m) (5,248ft/1,600m vertical)

LENGTH OF RUN:
3.1 miles (5km)

AVERAGE TIME:
60 minutes

AVALANCHE KIT:
Essential

ALTITUDE RANGE: 2,693–10,824ft (821–3,300m)

SKIABLE AREA:
255-4 miles (412km)

RUNS: 115

LIFTS: 90

WEB:
alpineguide.ch
verbier.ch
4valleys.ch

GETTING THERE:
Geneva (99.2 miles/160km),
Zurich (186 miles/300km)

SWITZERLAND

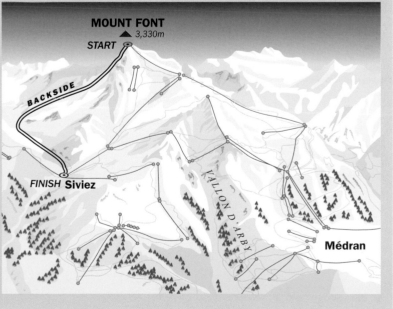

MOUNT FONT
▲ 3,330m
START

BACKSIDE

FINISH Siviez

KALLON D'ARBY

Médran

Diavolezza Glacier
St. Moritz, Switzerland
10,834ft (3,303m)

F amed for its high peaks and majestic scenery, Switzerland is chock-full of runs that provide amazing views and plenty of challenge. But one run claims to be the longest high-altitude glacier run of all in the country where winter-sports vacations began 150 years ago, and it's a bit of a stunner. It also turns out to be only a few miles away from where those first vacationmakers arrived at the Kulm Hotel in St. Moritz for the winter of 1864–65.

Switzerland's longest glacier run wasn't open back when those first winter tourists arrived, of course. Nor had the Alpine technique of downhill skiing been devised, for that matter, and wouldn't be for another 40 years, although the first downhill technique, telemark, was taking off in Norway around then thanks to the efforts of Sondre Norheim.

It takes just a few minutes for the modern cable car to whisk you to the top of this 6.2-mile (10-km) descent. In terms of gradient this run, sometimes known by its destination, the Morteratsch run, is around about a red classification, but unpisted of course, so much of the challenge depends on the conditions. There is also one 984-ft (300-m) stretch at the start that is steeper than the rest—a definite black—for which concentration is needed. If there has been heavy use of the slope, moguls can build toward the end of the day, adding to the challenge. Another major distraction is the awe-inspiring glacial scenery and the vast mountain panoramas, including the famed Piz Palü.

A very black run
After that first steep section, there is a traverse along the natural amphitheater across the Pers and Morteratsch glaciers before a second rapid drop in the terrain that can be very challenging when mogulled. If we were using the North American scale, it would be a definite double black diamond; perhaps "very black" is the best description for the Alps. Another flatter section with views back to the Bernina Mountains then follows, before a final steep section at the end of the glacier. A cross-country trail then leads you back to the railwroad station in Morteratsch, from which you can take the train back to the ski lifts. The descent typically takes some 45 minutes and can be tackled without a guide, but it is still wise to be prepared for all conditions, and you should be skilled on steep, ungroomed terrain.

If you do hire a guide from the local Pontresina Mountaineering School, you'll find that there are many more off-piste routes to try in the area that should only be attempted in the company of a local expert.

This is also a wise choice if visibility is not good on the day you plan to tackle the descent. This is high-mountain glacier terrain: there are no safe alternative routes down and if rescue is required, it's only possible with a helicopter. So if in doubt, don't do it. In any case, on bad-weather days there are more groomed pistes in the small-but-perfectly-formed and inter-linked Diavolezza–Lagalb region, and the full 217 miles (350km) of runs included on the Engadin pass to enjoy, too.

Diavolezza is known as one of the three St. Moritz ski areas, but is in fact a 30-minute bus ride from the world-famous resort and rather closer to the more low-key choice of Pontresina. It does not matter much in terms of your lift ticket, as all three, and half a dozen more ski areas in the region, as well as rail and bus transportation between them, are included in the Engadin regional pass.

The glacier of the she-devil
As you ski down you can ponder the legend of Diavolezza, which means "female devil" in the local Romansh dialect, with the glacier named after a beautiful but malevolent fairy who lured local hunters to their deaths in her glacial crevasses. Those crevasses are still there and the lift company will warn you against skiing off the Diavolezza trail (which is marked and secured from avalanche) without a guide, for fear of succumbing to the same fate. The bad fairy, according to the legend, decided to leave when the glacier reached the valley, covering her domain in ice. Whether global warming will bring her back again is anyone's guess.

One option to make the run even more special is to spend the previous night on the mountain. The Berghaus Diavolezza, 9,840ft (3,000m) up at the top of the lifts, offers a variety of accommodation from twin en-suite rooms to dorms, where you can stay overnight, thus being first on the run the next morning. Once the day-skiers leave the slopes by 5 p.m., you can watch the sunset on the high peaks and glaciers of the Bernina Alps before tucking into specialties the chef has cooked up from the local Graubünden region or from just over the border in Italy's Valtellina. There's also the option of taking a dip in the highest-altitude hot tub in Europe. It's one of the warmest, too, heated to 106°F (41°C), as the water cools more quickly than usual once the lid's off because of the altitude.

So a great run, through spectacular scenery and a gourmet meal, then a hot-tub dip at sunset. All the ingredients of a perfect day? But watch out for that malevolent fairy.

Fact file Diavolezza Glacier

IN SHORT: The devil's run is a remarkably heavenly experience

TOUGHNESS:
☠☠☠

FEAR FACTOR:
☠☠

VERTICAL: 9,751–6,153ft (2,973–1,876m) (3,598ft/1,097m vertical)

AVERAGE TIME:
45 minutes

LENGTH OF RUN:
5.6 miles (9km)

ACCESS: Cable car

BEST TIME: February–May

AVALANCHE KIT:
Essential

ALTITUDE RANGE: 5,642–10,834ft (1,720–3,303m)

SKIABLE AREA:
217 miles (350km)

RUNS: 88

LIFTS: 56

WEB:
diavolezza.ch
mountains.ch

GETTING THERE: Milan (124 miles/200km), Zurich (130.2 miles/210km)

SWITZERLAND

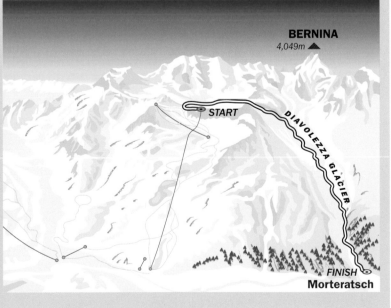

BERNINA
4,049m ▲

START

DIAVOLEZZA GLACIER

FINISH
Morteratsch

The Wall/Paradise
Champéry, Switzerland
8,088ft (2,466m)

When I was a novice skier, first seeking out the challenges to be had on the slopes of Europe, I was intrigued when a friend asked me if I had ever heard of a brown run. I tried to sound knowledgeable—I knew of green, blue, red, and black runs, I said, I knew that the German-speaking eastern Alps did not hold with greens and only used the other three colors to grade their runs, I knew that across the Atlantic there were no reds and runs had symbols as well as colors—green squares, blue circles, black diamonds; sometimes double and even triple black diamonds. But in the end I had to admit I had never heard of a brown run. My friend insisted he knew of one, lying just on the Swiss side of the French border. It was called The Wall and it was a brown run, he laughed, because that was the effect it had on your pants as you stood at the summit and peered over the top. Well, we were teenage boys.

The Wall, also known as The Swiss Wall, or, if you are actually Swiss, Le Mur Suisse or Le Pas de Chavanette, is a vast, precipitous mogul field that's sadly not shown in brown on the piste map of the Portes du Soleil. This is a huge ski region of some 403 miles (650km) of runs above a dozen or so French and Swiss villages, most of them lift-linked to one another and including famous resort names such as Avoriaz, Champéry, Châtel, Les Gets, and Morzine. You can access The Wall from any of these, but it's closest to Avoriaz. About two-thirds of the region lies on the French side of the border, the remainder on the Swiss.

Hitting The Wall

As with so many runs, just how bad The Wall is to ski on the day that you arrive is down, in most part, to the conditions. If it's cold and it has not snowed in weeks, those massive moguls will be icy, and the likelihood of a long bumpy slide if you lose an edge is high. On the other hand, arrive after a moderate fresh snowfall with temperatures just a little below zero and the challenge may be lessened and the pleasure increased (unless you actually like icy moguls on a super-steep slope where you can pretty much bump your helmet on the mogul above you as you stand up and lean in to the vertical).

This variation means that you will get different viewpoints (again, as with all great runs) as to whether The Wall is overrated or whether it is indeed the most formidable run of the 28 rated black in the Portes du Soleil. Those who say, "Been there, done that" when belittling the

Fact file The Wall/Paradise

IN SHORT: A rare brown run—you peer over the top and feel its effect presently

TOUGHNESS:
☠☠☠☠

FEAR FACTOR:
☠☠☠☠

VERTICAL:
7,219–5,966ft (2,201–1,819m) (597ft/182m vertical)

AVERAGE TIME:
45 minutes

LENGTH OF RUN:
5.6 miles (9km)

ACCESS: Chairlift

BEST TIME: All season

AVALANCHE KIT:
Nonessential

ALTITUDE RANGE: 2,624–8,088ft (800–2,466m)

SKIABLE AREA:
403 miles (650km)

RUNS: 286

LIFTS: 195

WEB:
portesdusoleil.com

GETTING THERE:
Geneva (49.6 miles/80km)

SWITZERLAND

DENT BLANCHE
▲ 2,756m

COL DU FORNET

POINTE DE RIPAILLE

CHAVANETTE
START

THE WALL

FINISH

POINTE DE VORLAZ

POINTE DE MOSSETTE

Avoriaz

mighty Wall are likely to speak of their preference for La Combe du Machon, considered a more "technically challenging" descent and just over a mile longer.

So what is the challenge of The Wall? Well the piste—essentially a wide open, fairly level slope above the treeline—pitches at up to 50 degrees over its 0.62-mile (1-km) length as it descends 1,312 vertical feet (400m).

But that pitch alone is not what forms The Wall's formidable reputation: it's those moguls, which can reach 7ft (2m) high. This all looks particularly bad at the top, as that's the steepest section, and many people opt to hop on the adjacent Chavanette chairlift, which runs the length of the slope and can be used for laps if you want to do it all over again when you reach the bottom. This chairlift is unusual in that it has about as many people riding down, craning to look over their right shoulders for fallers on the slope behind them, as are riding up.

An annual race down the slope saw the fastest descent record set at 20 seconds by extreme skier, Dominique Perret. Dominique also likes cliff jumping and set a record for jumping 125ft (38m) off a nearby rocky overhang in the Pas de Chavanette.

The paradise run

Once you do reach the bottom of The Wall, however, and find yourself at the head of a vast snowy expanse descending gently down toward the Swiss villages of Les Crosets, Champoussin, and Champéry, there is an unexpected reward. Hop on to the Ripaille lift waiting there and you'll be dragged to the top of the Grand Paradis (or "Paradise") run—another of the region's great descents, but a very different one.

The Paradise run begins with a wide, sweeping, easy, blue-graded run, then continues for 5 wonderful miles (8km) down into woodland and through spectacular isolation (although you do pass several enticing restaurants where you might stop and linger a while). The magnificent jagged peaks of the Dents du Midi (10,683ft/3,257m) tower above you to your right and there is seldom a soul in sight. It really lives up to its name.

The full descent from the top of The Wall to the bottom of Paradise takes in two countries and some 5.6 miles (9km) of skiing. It takes you from some of the steepest, most challenging marked pistes at the start to the most benign and relaxing of slopes at the end. It is a truly fabulous run.

Parsenn to Küblis
Davos, Switzerland
9,328ft (2,844m)

Although downhill skiing of the Alpine variety that we know today began in the first decade of the 20th century, people had been skiing downhill in the Alps for the last decade or so of the 19th century. They predominantly used skis of the newly invented telemark variety from Norway, which had caught the public imagination across Europe and the wider world.

Many of the early ski resorts have their tales of when the first pair of skis arrived in the village. One particularly good one from Grindelwald tells of an Englishman, Mr. Fox, who put his skis on in his hotel room, then clomped out through the lobby wearing them. The first skis arrived in Davos in 1883 when a German pharmacist, Mr. Paulcke, ordered a pair for his son who started skiing with his school friends. The interest in skiing was such that local wagon-maker, Tobias Branger, became the first Swiss producer of skis, importing a new design he saw at a Paris trade fair in 1889. Apparently the idea of moving around on 7-ft- (2-m-) long wooden skis was ridiculed by other villagers (another common theme in those early stories), so Mr. Branger initially skied under cover of darkness to avoid the public humiliation.

Things had turned around by 1894 when Sir Arthur Conan Doyle, creator of Sherlock Holmes, became the latest British writer to visit the resort (Robert Louis Stevenson, the writer of *Treasure Island* and *Dr. Jekyll and Mr. Hyde* had been in town for the winters of 1880–81 and 1881–82, but he was too early for skiing). Tobias Branger and his brother made the first winter crossing of the Maienfeld–Furka Pass to Arosa on March 23, 1893 and a year later skiing hit British headlines when Sir Arthur Conan Doyle accompanied the two brothers on the same trip in eight hours and then wrote up his adventure for *Strand* magazine in London. Skiing came out of the darkness.

The birthplace of Alpine skiing

So it is that Davos, along with western Austria's Arlberg and the little village of Lillienfeld near Vienna in the east, each of which can report a crucial "first" in the early years of skiing, can claim to be "the birthplace

In the tracks of pioneers

Parsenn is now the largest of six sectors of the largely lift-linked Davos–Klosters ski region (the others are Rinerhorn, Jakobshorn, Pischa, Parsenn, Madrisa, and Schatzalp). With 192.2 miles (310km) of piste it's a much easier trip these days, what with the lift up, maps, guides, and a trainline back from Küblis to Davos. It remains a classic, though, and to ski it you are following in the tracks of some of the very earliest pioneers.

The most challenging part of the descent across the massif normally comes at the very top of Weissfluhgipfel, which is rated black and is steep. The challenge can be exacerbated in the early morning if it's icy, so toward lunchtime or later can be a better time to start your run. After this, the wide trail turns to an intermediate red-level gradient and is pure pleasure as you head down toward the treeline. The lower section through the forest past Schifer is little more than a track toward the valley floor, but overall still worthy of your attention.

of Alpine skiing." Davos also went on to become one of the world's great ski towns, famous even beyond winter sports as the host each January of the World Economic Forum, drawing together presidents and other world leaders, top industrialists, and many more in a global think tank, sometimes with a bit of skiing thrown in.

But Davos has another claim—one of the oldest ski runs in the world, just coming up to 120 years old, in fact. Inspired by Conan Doyle, four more pioneering ski tourists lost their way up on the 8,731-ft (2,662-m) Weissfluhjoch trying to copy Conan Doyle's trip to Arosa and, after a night sleeping rough in a hut they found, ultimately found themselves in the hamlet of Küblis, in the process discovering one of the world's great ski runs, a 7.4-mile- (12-km-) long, off-piste descent from Parsenn. Of course everything was off-piste then, but this descent is still off-piste today.

The run became more established from 1904 and even more so from 1931, when the first true skier's funicular railroad was built up to the Weissfluhjoch. Access became easier still on December 10, 1955 when the gondola to the 9,328 ft (2,844-m) Weissfluhgipfel opened, enabling an effortless approach to the full run down to Küblis.

On of the longest descents in the world

There are many variants on the most famous run to Küblis, including one option that takes you instead round to that favorite resort of British royals, Klosters. Some variants are steeper and some longer, and the local ski school and mountain guides will be happy to explore the possibilities with you. One of the longest such descents in the world is an 11.2-mile (18-km) run to more neighboring hamlets, Fideris and Jenaz, with the chance to catch the train back to Davos at the end. Each, however, requires a climb with skins on your skis from the Kreuzweg on Parsenn to the Strassberger Furggli to begin the long descent. There are also several more sections with climbs and traverses, so it is not quite constant downhill.

Conveniently, all these runs and the train rides that take you back to your base are included in one regional lift pass. And another aspect of the runs that's better now than in the 1890s is that the enterprising owners of chalets *en route* sometimes turn them into cafés for passing skiers to stop for refreshment. Sherlock Holmes would surely approve.

Fact file Parsenn to Küblis

IN SHORT: One of the world's oldest ski runs and still one of the best

TOUGHNESS: ☠☠

FEAR FACTOR: ☠☠

VERTICAL: 9,328–2,657ft (2,844m–810m) (6,672ft/2,034m vertical)

AVERAGE TIME: One hour

LENGTH OF RUN: Approx. 8 miles (13km)

ACCESS: Parsenn funicular

BEST TIME: February–May

AVALANCHE KIT: Essential

ALTITUDE RANGE: 5,117–9,328ft (1,560–2,844m)

SKIABLE AREA: 192.2 miles (310km)

RUNS: 85

LIFTS: 56

WEB: davos.ch

GETTING THERE: Zurich (99.8 miles/161km) or by train to Davos

SWITZERLAND

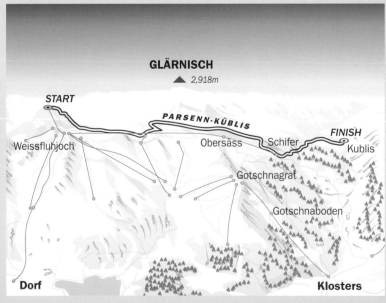

GLÄRNISCH
▲ 2,918m

START

PARSENN-KÜBLIS

FINISH

Weissfluhjoch

Obersäss   Schifer

Kublis

Gotschnagrat

Gotschnaboden

Dorf

Klosters

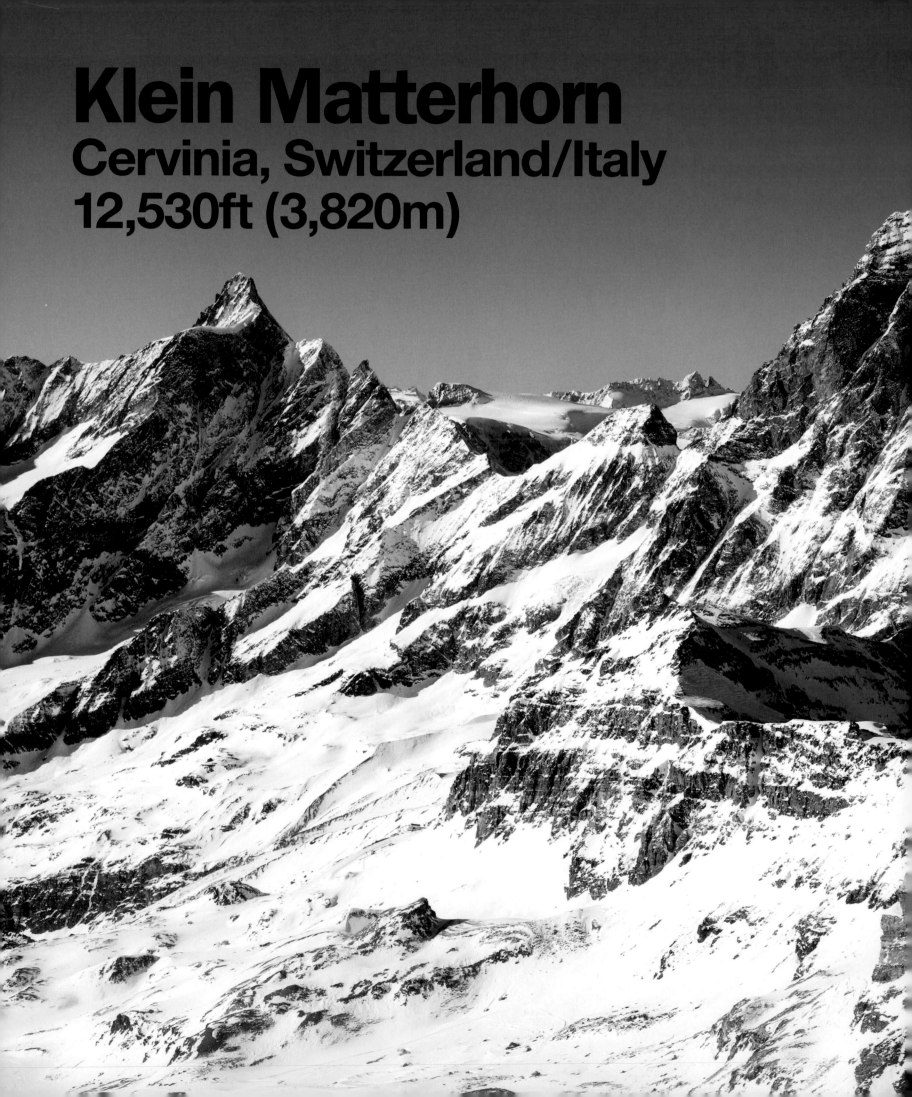

Klein Matterhorn
Cervinia, Switzerland/Italy
12,530ft (3,820m)

Europe's highest lift-served slopes are accessed from the Klein Matterhorn (far left, with Matterhorn on the left), just on the Swiss side of the Italian border, which you can ski right through.

At 12,789ft (3,899m), the highest ski lift in Europe runs right by the Swiss/Italian border, high above Zermatt and Breuil-Cervinia. This lift to the highest point at Goba di Rollin crowns what also appears, at first sight of the stats, to be the biggest lift-served vertical drop in the world. You can, it seems, descend 7,790 vertical feet (2,375m) from the top of that draglift to the village of Valtournenche at 4,999ft (1,524m) all in one go.

Well, nearly. As is so often the case with these claimants of world-record ski stats, there are a few provisos. Zermatt, along with Austria's Hintertux glacier, is one of only two resorts open for snowsports, weather permitting, 365 days a year, and that lift to 12,789ft (3,899m) only operates in the summer. At that point the bottom half of the vertical is green, lush, and filled with marmots chomping on the beautiful Alpine flowers, but not great for skiing. So when you walk through the 328-ft- (100-m-) long tunnel at the top of the Klein Matterhorn cable car and come out gasping a bit with the altitude, you'll start your descent 259 vertical feet (79m) lower at a mere 12,530ft (3,820m) above sea level (purists, also known as "ski nerds," will point out that the official Zermatt winter ski area stat of 12,740ft/3,884m is for the top of the viewing platform, not the height of the ski run). Your vertical is thus diminished to a mere 7,531 vertical feet (2,296m).

But that 12,530ft (3,820ft) is still Europe's highest ski-run start and one of the eight highest in the world. The Vallée Blanche quotes 12,602ft (3,842m), but again that's the viewing platform on the Aiguille du Midi. The top of the cable car is 12,431ft (3,790m) and once you've edged down the arête carrying your skis or board, you're at around 12,234ft (3,730m).

But above Zermatt the stats for the vertical get worse. The vertical distance between the top of the lift at Zermatt and the bottom at Valtournenche cannot quite be skied in one, continuous, glorious descent—a short draglift link is required halfway down the 9.2-mile (14.8-km) run. How tiresome. In fact the longest, continuous, skiable vertical is down to the base of the Matterhorn Express, the high-speed lift that whisks you much of the way up this mighty mountain from Zermatt itself at 5,346ft (1,630m) (again

a little different to the official figure, 5,314ft/1,620m which is for Zermatt's village church, which you can't ski to), a total of "only" 7,183 vertical feet (2,190m).

And after that simple explanation, it must be time to start skiing.

Let's take in that summit view first after the usually cramped cable-car ride up to the Klein Matterhorn. The views of the Matterhorn proper are, of course, spectacular from right down in Zermatt and just get more jaw-dropping the higher you climb. There are many descents possible from the Klein Matterhorn and, as is often the case, it is tricky to decide on one run only. There are perhaps more challenging off-piste options available by staying on the Swiss side and heading down to Zermatt, or you may prefer a run such as Triftji on the Gornergrat, one of the longest mogul slopes in the world. My favorite, however, is the long, cruising red that sweeps across the border into Italy and down to Breuil-Cervinia, not least because on busy days you find yourself free of the crowds as soon as you pass the border marker at Plateau Rosa. The cafés turn from large, corporate, highway service station-style establishments to small, family-run options, and you'll find that a homemade espresso is a third of the price of a self-service machine at Trockner Steg.

With that skier's left-turn off the Plateau Rosa, you feel almost like you have found a secret door off the beaten piste, and a wondrous, incredibly long, wide piste opens up below you for pure high-speed cruising pleasure. It's feels something like when you're driving across America and a vast, open highway stretching to the horizon appears in front of you after leaving a city— so just ski it and enjoy it.

Stop and smell the coffee

Do stop for a real Italian coffee once you've got a few miles under your skis. A particularly good place to stop for your espresso, and indeed your lunch, is the Grand Sometta, a favorite of the jockey Frankie Dettori. It's a cozy wooden hut of the classic mountain variety, family-run with truly homemade daily specials that the waitress will dictate to you off the top of her head. You can forget all your vast cafeterias at the top of the gondolas, or indeed your overpriced, silver-service gourmet mountain restaurants: this is the real deal.

Then it's back on the piste for another 3.1 or 3.7 miles (5–6km) of cruising down to Breuil-Cervinia.

Let's end back at those numbers. At worst, you've just skied the seventh biggest lift-served continual vertical in the world—but most of the six above have their own "issues" that may disqualify them, so it depends where you draw the line. And besides, if you sweet talk the lift company, as celebrated German ski writer Christoph Schrahe managed to, they'll run that summer draglift at the top for you in winter anyway.

LEFT: Skiing with the mighty Matterhorn on your horizon is one of the most magical experiences in snowsports.

RIGHT: The run down from the Klein Matterhorn is one very long cruise on blue- and red-gradient terrain, but if that's still not enough for you and you want to spice it up a bit, you can always jump into the powder at the side of the run and grab some air.

Fact file Klein Matterhorn

IN SHORT: One of the longest groomed runs in the world, and you ski across the border, too

TOUGHNESS: ☠☠

FEAR FACTOR: ☠☠

VERTICAL: 12,530-6,724ft (3,820-2,050m) (5,806ft/1,770m vertical)

AVERAGE TIME: 45 mins

LENGTH OF RUN: 7.1 miles (11.5km)

ACCESS: Klein Matterhorn

cable car

BEST TIME: Dec–April

AVALANCHE KIT: Nonessential

ALTITUDE RANGE: 4,999-12,530ft (1,524–3,820m)

SKIABLE AREA: 217 miles (350km) (Cervinia–Zermatt International Ski Area)

RUNS: 150 (Cervinia–Zermatt International Ski Area)

LIFTS: 56 (Cervinia–Zermatt International

Ski Area)

WEB: zermatt.ch cervinia. it**GETTING THERE:** Zermatt: Zurich (74.4 miles/120km); Breuil-Cervinia: Turin (73.2 miles/118km)

SWITZERLAND

ITALY

BREITHORN
▲ 4,165m

START

GORNERGLETSCHER

KLEIN MATTERHORN ROUTE

Furi

Breuil-Cervina

FINISH

Olympia
Cortina d'Ampezzo, Italy
9,640ft (2,939m)

Ski areas come in all shapes and sizes, but few tick as many boxes as Cortina d'Ampezzo in Italy.

As you arrive in the resort, you are most likely to be impressed first by the spectacular beauty of the massive Dolomite peaks that tower above the village, their vast precipices of sheer rock shining pink in the sunlight from the horizon at dawn and dusk. This typical Dolomite phenomenon is called *Alpenglühen* (Alpenglow) and wonderfully, that pinkiness is in large part down to the fact that some 60 million years ago these were vast coral reefs lying under prehistoric seas, before the land was heaved up. It's right that these are now recognized as a UNESCO World Natural Heritage Site.

If you then take a walk along the central Corso Italia, lined with enticing stores and restaurants, it's equally likely that you will be rapidly absorbed into *la dolce vita*—the happy, relaxed lifestyle with which Cortina is infused. The resort has a timeless quality and there is none of the feeling of rapid growth in the 1960s and 1970s that is so evident at many other world-famous resorts. Cortina has grown, of course, but always with style.

There has been skiing here since 1925, and what skiing! There are three main ski areas surrounding the resort and they, in turn, connect to the massive Dolomiti Superski lift-pass system, with more than 744 miles (1,200km) of piste spread over a dozen neighboring ski regions, together served by almost 450 lifts.

Groomed or off-piste—take your pick

The three main local areas (along with several smaller options) are Tofana, Faloria–Cristallo, and Lagazuoi Cinque Torri, which between them offer around 99.2 miles (160km) of piste and are each reached by classic cable-car ascents. The variety of terrain surrounding the resort is vast, and choosing the best run, therefore, will always be a matter of debate. Unlike many great resorts where the choice is so difficult, Cortina has both splendid, groomed runs to consider and also spectacular off-piste descents.

In the former category I was sorely tempted by the wonderful "Hidden Valley" descent, a remarkable blue/red run of about 5 miles (8km) in length from Lagazuoi (9,020ft/2,750m), itself reached by the unusual (the doors close vertically) cable car up from Passo Falzarego, a 20-minute bus ride from Cortina's center.

The Hidden Valley is so called because, after the 360-degree views from the terrace of the Lagazuoi refuge at the top, it carves its way through vast and towering Dolomitic structures, passing frozen waterfalls that somehow give it a secret, private feel. Indeed, it's rare that you come across more than a handful of other skiers on the run.

Before you do descend, though, take time to stop for lunch at the Lagazuoiv refuge, established in 1965 and still run by the Pompanin family of mountain guides. If they're open, take a quick tour of the century-old tunnels carved in the rock by the defending

LEFT: Plunging down through the treeline, the Olympia run has been graced by many of the world's best skiers over the decades, including Austrian skier Tony Sailer, who won three gold medals in the 1956 Winter Games.

Italian army a century ago, during the First World War. There's no lift back up from the end of the Hidden Valley; instead, you can join one of two lines of skiers towed behind ponies to make the novel, literally "horse-powered" connection to Alta Badia and another great name in Italian skiing, the Sella Ronda circuit. This is 27.3 miles (44km) of lifts and runs linking in total perhaps 310 miles (500km) of runs around Val Gardena, Badia, and Fassa—probably the world's second biggest lift-linked area, though never marketed as such. Or you can jump into a shared minibus back to Passo Falzarego.

ABOVE: As soon as you arrive in Cortina, the dramatic scenery of the Dolomites dominates the skyline.

The ultimate Cortina classic

But a decision on the very best run had to be made, and in the end I decided to be true to Cortina's competitive roots and its Olympic heritage (it hosted the Winter Games of 1956) and choose the classic Olympia piste on the Tofane, on the northwest side of the Ampezzo valley, just under the magnificent Tofane massif.

Olympia, which still appears on our TV screens each year as the Women's World Cup downhill run, when the racers scream through its narrow rock walls, is a Cortina classic epitomizing everything that's great about skiing here. In 1956, the great Austrian skier Tony Sailer surprised himself by winning gold in all three speed events contested at the Games (downhill, slalom, and giant slalom). It's also proclaimed by the resort itself as being "The most famous piste in Italy!"—and who could argue with that?

In short, it's the run that has everything—length, challenge, scenery, fame, history, glamour, and that mainstay of Italian skiing, great restaurants to stop off at as you descend (assuming you're not representing your country in the downhill at the time).

Olympia is located on the Tofana di Mezzo, the middle and highest of the three peaks of the Tofana sector. The descent begins from the top of the Duca d'Aosta–Pomedes triple chair fed by the Rumerlo–Duca d'Aosta quad—or alternatively via the lift system from Socrepes, or even the Tofana cable car from the Col Druscie station, then skiing down.

After a comparatively gentle first few hundred feet, your stomach drops into the very steep "Schuss" black section before skirting the area of the Duca d'Aosta mountain restaurant, where the Olympic flame was kept safe before the opening ceremony in 1956. Racers hit a circling jump and then "the great S-bends" before the run descends below the treeline toward the "Bus de ra Pales" and finally onto the Pale of Rumerlo. You could perhaps take it at a slightly gentler pace; after all, that's the more relaxed, Italian way.

Fact file Olympic

IN SHORT: The great descent from the racy queen of the Dolomites, boasting maximum length, speed, glamour, and history —James Bond would and did approve

TOUGHNESS:
☠☠☠

FEAR FACTOR:
☠☠☠

VERTICAL:
7,642–5,117ft
(2,330–1,560m)

(2,526ft/770m vertical)

AVERAGE TIME: 2 mins

LENGTH OF RUN:
2,899yds (2,660m)

ACCESS: Duca d'Aosta–Pomedes chairlift

BEST TIME: All season

AVALANCHE KIT: Minimal

ALTITUDE RANGE:
4,015–9,640ft (1,224–2,939m)

SKIABLE AREA: 99.2 miles (160km) (Dolomiti Superski: 756.4 miles/1,220km)

RUNS: 70

LIFTS: 37
(Dolomiti Superski: 444)

WEB:
dolomiti.org

GETTING THERE:
Venice (99.2 miles/160km)

ITALY

START

OLYMPIA

CORTINA

FINISH

Balma
Alagna, Italy
10,693ft (3,260m)

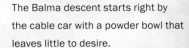

The Balma descent starts right by the cable car with a powder bowl that leaves little to desire.

T he world's most famous 6,560-ft- (2,000-m-) plus, lift-served verticals are Chamonix in France at 9,184ft (2,800m), Zermatt in Switzerland at 7,544ft (2,300m), and Alagna in Italy at 6,724ft (2,050m).

Alagna, in the country's northwest, up near the French and Swiss borders. You must know it? Sixty years ago, they built that three-stage lift from the village up to Punta Indren at 10,693ft (3,260m), with a tow lift taking you higher still, on up to 11,644ft (3,550m), opening up one of the world's biggest lift-served verticals (in fact you can climb another 3,280 vertical feet/1,000m higher, ski touring or with a helicopter).

The one thing they forgot when they built those lifts was to build more than a couple of runs back down. The result: freeride nirvana—an Italian version of La Grave, but with limited financial success. The latter factor wasn't a problem for the ski bums who arrived, eventually, in the '80s and '90s when word at last got out, in publications such as the skier's magazine *Powder,* of locals tackling 60-degree pitches before breakfast.

"The Italian Three Valleys"

Most of those locals weren't too bothered. The old Walser village had remained much the same for eight centuries, and while first gold miners, then 19th-century grand tourists and finally Italy's royal family had come and gone, their ancient wooden houses stood little changed.

But the powers-that-be were concerned. One of the most impressive ski areas in the world was not reaching its full potential and their answer was to replace those now-old cable cars with gondolas and chairlifts and, more importantly, to connect Alagna to the Aosta valley villages of Gressoney and Champoluc by a network of new lifts to form the Monterosa ski area, with the tagline "The Italian Three Valleys."

This has nearly all happened since 2000 and was completed just a few seasons ago when tens of millions of euros were spent on the final few state-of-the-art lifts while the rest of the world's ski industry tightened their belts postworldwide economic crash. The only change is that the top lift has now gone and the lifts peak at 10,742ft (3,275m).

BELOW: The lifts climb steeply from Alagna to open up one of the world's largest verticals.

RIGHT: Alagna has something to offer all abilities—some low-lying, easy, groomed runs as well as phenomenal precipitous terrain that provides plunging, black pistes.

The good news for freeride lovers is that they haven't cut many new ski runs. Although the local Milanese in-the-know arrive each weekend from the country's most fashionable city, the masses of destination skiers are still not booking packages to Alagna in great numbers. On the Alagna side, the steep landscape means Monterosa can still only offer the two extremes—some low-lying, easy, groomed runs or phenomenal steep, plunging, black piste and freeride terrain, and little in between.

To ascend some 10,824 vertical feet (3,300m) above Alagna, most people make their way up to the dramatic Rifugio Margherita, at 14,944ft (4,556m) claiming to be the world's highest. It is named after the queen who was the wife of Italy's King Umberto I of the Savoie, and a lover of high-mountain hiking in the area. She made it up there in 1893—the year that it opened.

From the Rifugio you can look across to the peaks of the Matterhorn and Mont Blanc and, deposited there by helicopter in the morning, begin that incredible descent. Be warned, however, that the descent is no Vallée Blanche (the world's longest, but also largely flat run down to Chamonix): it is a very, very steep descent with pitches of up to 50 degrees through wild, icy terrain suiting serious skiers, fully equipped with avalanche transceivers and other equipment, accompanied by a guide, and ideally with some mountaineering experience of their own. But then

that's the main appeal, too. If you don't want to climb so high, a descent of around 6,724 vertical feet (2,050m) is possible by taking that new highest lift to Punta Indren. To access this itinerary, known as Balma, it is a 10–15-minute traverse and a climb of about 82 vertical feet (25m) to get around the ridge that separates the lift's top station from the Alagna descent. If snow conditions are good, you can then ski all the way down to the village.

Alagna's lack of mass-market appeal has so far limited the development of luxury lodging and, unless you're satisfied with something as rough and ready as the slopes above, you might opt to stay in one of the neighboring villages now linked by ski lifts and runs. Over on this more user-friendly Aosta valley side, the villages are as yet largely unspoilt, too—but, with a bigger share of the region's 99.2 miles (160km) or so of easy and intermediate pistes, they are drawing bigger crowds, and businesses are able to flourish and develop.

So those centuries-old, dark wooden Walser houses still remain largely untainted by adjacent concrete-condo complexes. The steep slopes remain largely deserted mid-week and unchanged from how they were in the 1950s, and no doubt the 1850s before anyone thought to ski down them—steep and snowy, and enormous fun.

Fact file Balma

IN SHORT: A very steep descent of up to 50 degrees through wild, icy terrain suited only to serious skiers

TOUGHNESS:
☠☠☠☠

FEAR FACTOR:
☠☠☠☠

VERTICAL: 10,693–3,969ft (3,260–1,210m) (6,724ft/2,050m vertical)

AVERAGE TIME: Two hours

LENGTH OF RUN: 3.1 miles (5km)

ACCESS: Lifts, touring or helicopter

BEST TIME: Spring, usually

AVALANCHE KIT: Essential

ALTITUDE RANGE: 3,969–10,693ft (1,210–3,260m)

SKIABLE AREA: 111.6 miles (180km) (Monterosa)

RUNS: 61 (Monterosa)

LIFTS: 31 (Monterosa)

WEB: alagna.it
monterosa-ski.com

GETTING THERE: Milan (68.2 miles/110km)

ITALY

PUNTA DUFOUR
4,633m ▲

START   BALMA

Stafal-Tschaval

FINISH

Alagna

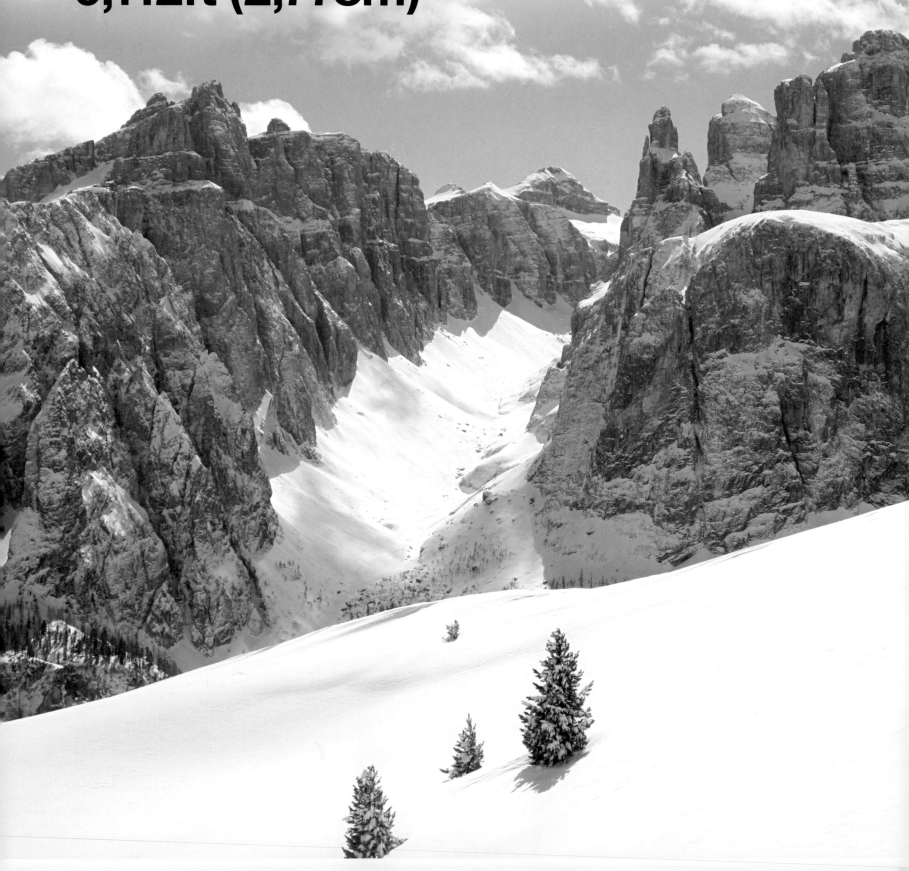

Val de Mesdì
Alta Badia, Italy
9,112ft (2,778m)

Alta Badia, home to half a dozen resort villages including little Colfosco, is one in a string of resorts and valleys that interconnect around the huge Sella Massif in the heart of the Dolomiti Superski region. It is possible to ski around this massive mountain, with its precipitous sides, in one direction or another on largely easy trails and, these days, riding comfortable chairlifts. The runs add up to around 14.3 miles (23km) and there's another 8.7 miles (14km) of lifts to make the full circuit.

The alternative to Dolomiti Superski

It's a great experience skiing from Alta Badia, on above Val Gardena and Val di Fassa around to Arabba and then back to Alta Badia. Actually, if you add together all the linked terrain that connects to the core circuit, some estimates have calculated that around 310 miles (500km) of trails are interconnected, making this region second only to the French Trois Vallées.

In fact, a plan to link, more or less, Cortina d'Ampezzo's skiing in the next few years could take the tally up beyond 372 miles (600km) and potentially into the top spot. It's just that, with the area divided between the more Germanic region toward the Austrian border to the north and the more Italian resorts to the south, there seems little motivation to ever measure it properly and agree a joint marketing strategy. Instead, the onus is always on the larger Dolomiti Superski region, with over 744 miles (1,200km) of partly lift-linked piste spread over a dozen valleys.

In this case, however, size does not really matter anyway. The key draw is the marvelous scenery, protected by UNESCO World Heritage site status, with vast cliffs of pink Dolomitic rock towering improbably above the gentle valleys.

Too gentle is indeed a complaint of some hardcore skiers, who note that the valleys of the Dolomites are often classic U-shapes, with the upper sections unskiable vertical cliffs and the valley runs nearly flat, rather than the more classic V-shape of the Alps further north.

But for those who love the Dolomites, that only makes the great runs that do exist here all the more special. In most cases these are formed through fissures in those high cliff walls, which are wide enough—often only just wide enough—for a run. Gradients, limited terrain, and other natural hazards can often make them unskiable, but again the rarity of being able to descend only adds to the allure.

Just such a run, and the most famous of several popular freeride itineraries of the Sella group, is the infamous Val de Mesdì, which arrives down in Colfosco, although you actually begin your day with a departure on the Arabba side of the Sella Massif.

The run is accessed by the Pordoi cable car, which departs close to Arabba, from the top of which is a 40–60-minute crossing to the other side of Sassol Pordoi. Depending on conditions it may be possible to hike this, but otherwise skins are advisable and whatever the conditions the route is not recommended without a professional guide, some degree of avalanche awareness training, off-piste experience, and being in possession of full backcountry gear—transceiver, probe, shovel; the works.

Cross from the top of the lift at Rifugio Maria (9,676ft/2,950m) down to the Rifugio Forcella Pordoi (9,279ft/2,829m) and continue along the great plateau to the Rifugio Boe (closed in winter), and along the northern slopes of the rocky pyramid that is Piz Boé (10,339ft/3,152m). It's especially important to be aware of how stable the snowpack is at this point.

Here the Val de Mesdì begins, with the opening facing in a northeasterly direction and the imposing Tower Berger, on the left, marking the beginning of the descent itself. Far below at the bottom of the gorge, you can see Colfosco waiting for you.

As with so many of the classic off-piste itineraries that have made the cut and been included in this book, it's the initial, steepest section of the run that's the most challenging. The slope pitches at around 35 degrees and the rock walls tower high above you, meaning that relatively tight turns are required.

But again, like many of the other steep descents, the slope eases out considerably quite quickly as you descend, and you can relax and take in the magnificent views. The only really crucial advice is to avoid going too far to the left where there are large rock hazards, but your guide will lead the way.

Pick your time

Choosing a time to make the run can be problematic. You need enough snow for conditions to be good right to the bottom, otherwise you may face a bit of hiking at the end on the flatter sections close to the valley floor (you should eventually ski past a few trees out onto a groomed piste). On the other hand, too much snow can make an unstable snowpack more likely. You also need a clear day to be able to make the most of the spectacular views.

For those who think this run is too tame, there are several more options that guides can take you to if you have the technical ability. These "north-side couloirs" are steeper than the classic itinerary, with 45–50-degree pitches and still narrower entrances, sometimes made more complicated by cornices. Ropes are often required for safe descents.

Whichever way you go, once you're back in Alta Badia you can smugly reflect on the fact that you're one of the small percentage of people to have skied across the Sella Ronda, rather than just the normal routes clockwise or counterclockwise around it.

TOP LEFT: The challenge of Val de Mesdì varies with the snow conditions; perfect in powder, it can test your limits if icy.
RIGHT: The steep slope and undulating terrain means that you can get airborne if you wish and have scoped your landing spot.

Fact file Val de Mesdì

IN SHORT: Why go around the great Sella Ronda when you can cut across it?

TOUGHNESS:
☠☠☠☠☠

FEAR FACTOR:
☠☠☠☠☠

VERTICAL: 9,184–5,248ft (2,800–1,600m) (3,936ft/1,200m vertical)

AVERAGE TIME: 40 minutes

LENGTH OF RUN: 2.5 miles (4km)

ACCESS: Pordoi cable car

BEST TIME: February–May

AVALANCHE KIT: Essential

ALTITUDE RANGE: 4,343–9,115ft (1,324–2,778m)

SKIABLE AREA: 80.6 miles (130km) (Dolomiti Superski 756.4 miles/1,220km)

RUNS: 94

LIFTS: 54 (Dolomiti Superski 444)

WEB: altabadia.org

GETTING THERE: Innsbruck (93 miles/150km)

ITALY

PIZ BOÉ
▲ 3,151m

START

VAL DE MESDÌ

Colfosco

FINISH

Mount Etna
Sicily, Italy
8,541ft (2,604m)

LEFT: Europe's most active volcano, surrounded by the Mediterranean Sea, is perhaps not the most obvious location for a great ski run, but lifts have been built on each side and a full descent is a unique experience.

Although Sierra Nevada in southern Spain takes the title of "Europe's most southerly ski destination," the rather more unlikely choice of the continent's most active volcano, the infamous Mount Etna, runs it a close second on latitude.

Skiing on active volcanos is not unheard of: at one small Japanese ski area, skiing through volcanic steam is considered a novelty, and in South America the lift towers for the slopes on the Villarica volcano have rubber bungs in them to absorb regular ground vibrations. In June 2011, meanwhile, a 3.1-mile- (5-km-) long fissure in Chile's Puyehue–Cordón Caulle volcanic complex vented ash that fell as gray dust on the nearby ski slopes of Cerro Catedral and brought new meaning to the term "powder."

Playing with fire and ice

Given just how active Mount Etna has been in the past few decades, the Sicilians have taken maintaining their two ski areas on the mountain—Etna Nord at Linguaglossa and Etna Sud at Rifugio Sapienza —to extremes. In 1971 the first cable car built on the volcano was taken out by a lava flow, and a second cable car was damaged at Etna Sud in a 1983 eruption. However, 2002–03 was "the big one" when both ski

areas were destroyed in an eruption that was clearly visible from space and threw debris up to 372 miles (600km) away. George Lucas even sent a film crew over to get footage for part of the climactic scenes of his final *Star Wars* movie, *Revenge of the Sith*.

But since then lifts have been rebuilt once again and, despite its volatility, skiing on Mount Etna is generally regarded as relatively safe, so long as you're sensible. This is partly due to its vast size, which many do not appreciate. Covering an area of more than 386.1 square miles (1,000 sq km), its base is some 86.8 miles (140km) around and it towers to over 10,824ft (3,300m) high (the precise height, generally estimated at between 10,906 and 10,988 feet (3,325–3,350m), varies depending on seismic activity). It is commonly referred to as having four times the land mass of the nearby island nation of Malta.

Thus, considering the millions of visitors it receives year round, incidents are rare, the last reported in 1987 when a sudden explosion near the summit killed two tourists. It should be mentioned that lightning strikes are reported to have killed more people than volcanic activity below—the air near the summit can become highly charged in the frequent cloud cover. It's presumably the level of tourist interest that

Fact file **Mount Etna**

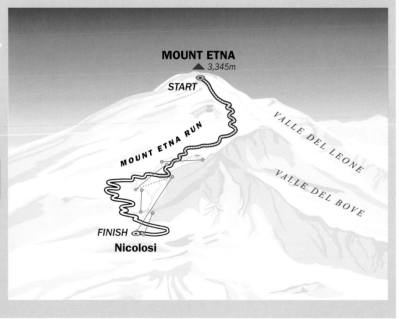

IN SHORT: Fire and ice

TOUGHNESS:
☠☠☠

FEAR FACTOR:
☠☠☠

VERTICAL: 10,939–
6,560ft (3,335–2,000m)
(4,379ft/1,335m vertical,
depending on conditions
at top and bottom)

AVERAGE TIME: One hour

LENGTH OF RUN:
Up to 3.1 miles (5km)

ACCESS: Ski lift; touring

BEST TIME: Usually
February (normally possible
from December–May)

AVALANCHE KIT:
Nonessential (but beware
of lava flow, volcanic
eruptions, and lightning)

ALTITUDE RANGE: 6,265–
8,541ft (1,910–2,604m)
(Etna Sud), 5,953–6,839ft
(1,815–2,085m) (Etna
Nord)

SKIABLE AREA: 4.2 miles
(6.7km) (Etna Sud), 3.1
miles (5km) (Etna Nord)
plus freeride

RUNS: 5 (Etna Sud), 5
(Etna Nord) plus freeride

LIFTS: 5 (Etna Sud),
4 (Etna Nord)

WEB: etnasci.it
funiviaetna.com
scuolaitalianascietna.it

GETTING THERE:
Catania (31 miles/50km)

ITALY

MOUNT ETNA
▲ *3,345m*

START

MOUNT ETNA RUN

VALLE DEL LEONE

VALLE DEL BOVE

FINISH
Nicolosi

makes rebuilding the lifts a worthwhile investment, and the latest is a gondola with cabins each able to carry eight passengers—hopefully it will remain intact between me writing this and you reading it.

But for our ski run, while we may use the lifts to gain some altitude the easy way, it is a case of climbing the extra 2,296–2,624 vertical feet (700–800m) in ski-touring gear to make the full descent. Pick a snowy winter and we may also be able to continue down further toward the Mediterranean Sea below the base of the groomed trails at the two ski centers.

Dance on a volcano

As you are ski touring and as Etna's terrain, and particularly what's skiable, is ever-changing depending on both seismic activity and snow cover, it is problematic to suggest a particular route in this instance and the "greatness" of the run is largely down to the novelty of skiing or boarding here. Good snow cover is required to make the rough terrain of solidified lava flows and ejected boulders skiable, but by spring the snow often lies several feet deep, so it's rarely a problem.

But that said, there are some great runs to be had if everything comes together, with several thousand feet of vertical possible on the barren mountainside. Both north and south sectors offer steep sections on upper slopes.

Although slopes lower down are typically more gentle, approximately equating to a blue category, there are rewards ahead as you ski closer to civilization and access the treeline. The terrain turns from desolate wilderness to pleasant skiing between birch and beech trees, then groves of orange, almond, and fig trees, so long as the snow cover lasts.

Weather permitting

Weather conditions can change rapidly, from benign Mediterranean sunshine with blue skies above and blue seas below to thick clouds and lightning storms, so skiing with a guide who can read the terrain and the weather is a must. They could perhaps take you for a ski past one of Etna's four main vents, usually emitting copious quantities of volcanic gas, for the full-on surreal-ski experience and show you the current best spots. Indeed the Italian SAGF (Soccorso Alpino Guardia di Finanza or Mountain Rescue Police) have released a list of ten pieces of essential advice for skiers on Etna, number one of which is don't ski alone. Number eight is also worth paying attention to: "Do not be fooled by the ease of access, Etna is a very dangerous mountain." The Etna Sci website provides full details of guiding services available, as well as an unusual "Etna Seismic Activity Report" next to the more usual "Etna Snow Report."

Your guide will lead you in safety to the summit (or as close as you can safely get), where you'll have the unique experience of views to the Ionian, Adriatic, and Mediterranean seas, the strong smell of sulfur, and the start of a ski run you'll never forget.

RIGHT: Lava streams are the least of your worries off-piste on Mount Etna; a guide is essential and lightning strikes one of the possible hazards.

Eastern Europe

Kanin to Sella Nevea
Slovenia/Italy
7,518ft (2,292m)

S kiing across a national border always feels rather special. There are perhaps a dozen places where ski lifts and groomed pistes make this easy to do in Europe, with famous options including two others included in this book—Switzerland to Italy from Zermatt to Cervinia (see pages 150–153), and France to Switzerland to reach The Wall in the Portes du Soleil (see pages 142–145). You could also ski from France to Italy from La Rosière to La Thuile, or from Austria to Switzerland on the "Duty Free" run from Ischgl to Samnaun. There is also the northerly Swedish center of Riksgränsen up in the Arctic Circle, famous for its skiing under the midnight sun in May and June each year. It includes one piste that famously stretches over the Norwegian border before returning back to Sweden at its base.

In years gone by, before the ridiculous idea that we might all get on if we were allowed to and border restrictions were relaxed, you could be stopped by skiing border-police when making one of these crossings and asked to produce your passport as well as your ski pass. That does still occasionally happen in Ischgl, apparently, as skiers returning from duty-free Samnaun can be stopped and have their backpacks searched, with any import duty due required for immediate payment or the confiscation of goods.

Through the Iron Curtain

In 2009 a new cross-border connection was made, the most easterly yet, linking the Slovenian ski area of Kanin to Sella Nevea in Italy. The resulting piste, Prevala, number seven on the map, is not, it must be admitted, quite the classic that most of the trails in this book are, although it does have much to recommend it. However, its inclusion is down to the great novelty of being able to ski through an invisible line that was once known as the Iron Curtain, the border between what was once Yugoslavia and Italy. This will particularly appeal to those of us of a certain age who spent our childhoods paranoid about imminent nuclear armageddon and nightly tales of people being shot as they tried to escape eastern Europe for the west.

Prevala can also often be noteworthy for its snow cover. In 2009 the region racked up one of the biggest snowfall accumulations in the world at 43ft (13m) for the season, the greatest reported that winter by any resort in Europe.

A different kind of courage is required these days to ski across the border from the former Eastern Block into Western Europe.

BELOW: The powder snow of southern Europe feels extra special after you've first looked out over the mountains to the Adriatric Sea.

RIGHT: Ski lifts now climb across the border that was once closed. Ride the lift from Italy into Slovenia, then ski back across.

The connection became reality when lift company Dopperlmayr installed a modern cable-car lift with cabins able to carry 100 passengers at a time. This bridged the gap across a high mountain valley on the Italian side, up to the Slovenian border where a quad chairlift awaits to take you to Sedlo (7,518ft/2,292m), the highest lift-served point in the country.

From here you may be able to get a glimpse of the Adriatic away to the west, as well as the jagged ridge of the Julian Alps stretching away north, a formidable natural border.

One option is to ski down into Slovenia and toward the city of Bovec far below in the Soda valley, rebuilt after the Second World War. In fact, sitting at less than 1,640ft (500m) above sea level, the huge vertical descent is not normally skiable all the way and the marked piste ends at the mid-station of the two-part gondola that brings skiers up from the town to the slopes.

Our descent, however, that piste number seven, plunges with glorious abandon through the high, treeless valley and veritable powder trap that cuts through the mountains and down into Italy. A good 738 vertical feet (225m) later we are crossing the border, although we may be sorely tempted, if skiing with a local guide and knowing that the snow is as deep as we're told, to take a right turn and drop into the off-piste itinerary of Krnica, a 4,297-ft (1,310-m) vertical descent that stays on the Slovenian side of the border and drops down through the forest.

Back on piste seven, the lower section offers more of the same as the run continues below the new cable car. If you take the triple chair at the end of the run it connects you with the latter half of the descent, around 2,624 vertical feet (800m) more down to the base of Sella Nevea.

Shortlisted for the Olympics

The Italian resort is very proud of its competitive credentials, being a regular Europa and World Cup host and also the venue of the Winter University Games in 2006, the year for which it was also shortlisted to stage the Olympics. The lower section of our descent takes us onto competition slopes from these various events.

A joint lift ticket covers the skiing on both sides of the border, and indeed week-long tickets extend the international mix skiable in the region to three countries: the ski areas of Arnoldstein and Nassfeld a little to the north, in Austria, are both included.

Fact file Kanin to Sella Nevea

IN SHORT: Ski through the Iron Curtain and see the sea

TOUGHNESS: ☠☠

FEAR FACTOR: ☠☠

VERTICAL:
7,518–3,608ft (2,292–1,100m) (3,910ft/1,192m vertical)

AVERAGE TIME: 30 mins

LENGTH OF RUN: 1.9 miles (3km)

ACCESS: Gondola, cable car, chairlift

BEST TIME:
January–April

AVALANCHE KIT:
Nonessential

ALTITUDE RANGE: 3,608–7,518ft (1,100–2,292m)

SKIABLE AREA:
31 miles (50km)

RUNS: 23

LIFTS: 14

WEB:
promotur.org
sellanevea.net
bovec.si boveckanin.si

GETTING THERE:
Ljubljana (43.4 miles/70km)

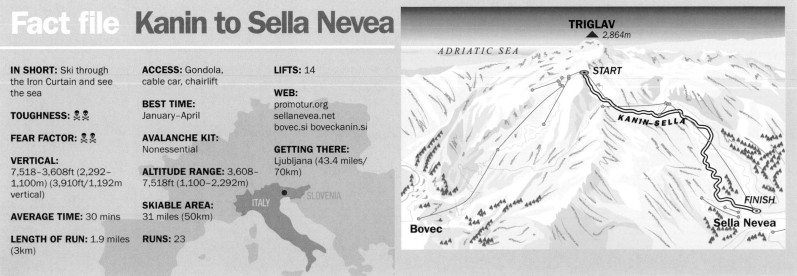

ITALY SLOVENIA

ADRIATIC SEA

TRIGLAV
▲ 2,864m

START

KANIN–SELLA

FINISH

Bovec

Sella Nevea

Goryczkowa
Zakopane, Poland
6,527ft (1,990m)

Why go west? The steep slopes of Zakopane have been attracting serious skiers since the turn of the 20th century.

It may come as a complete surprise for some, but there is a place in eastern Europe that ticks a lot of boxes for the discerning international winter-sport fanatic. Some might say there are better runs elsewhere in eastern Europe that should be in this book instead, and if your definition of a great ski run requires 6,560-ft (2,000-m) verticals, a precipitous powder slope, and perhaps a nice, fast gondola with heated seats to whisk you up the slopes, then I admit that the ski area of Kasprowy Wierch, one of about a dozen small ski areas close to the tourist town of Zakopane, will not be in your personal world top 50.

Call me romantic, but as I approach my twilight years and the cutting edge of the ski industry creates ever faster, more comfortable lifts reaching the tops of beautifully smooth, groomed pistes kept immaculate all season long thanks to snowmaking, I sometimes hark back to the early years of our sport, before snowmaking, before padded lifts, even before a full-day lift pass could be purchased. Zakopane provides all that and it also has a rich history that, for me, reflects the spread of downhill skiing outside those original resorts in the Alps to the wider world. It's something to reflect on as you ride the old wooden-seated chairlift to the top of the great Goryczkowa slope.

The most stunning vistas of the Tatras

Zakopane has become the largest and best-known tourist resort in Poland, as well as the country's highest city, albeit a small one with a population of less than 30,000. Originally a small mining settlement, it grew first as a spa town from the mid-19th century. Then the Skiers Association of Zakopane (Zakopiánski Oddział Narciarzy) was founded in 1907 and the first international ski competitions were staged in 1910, when Kasprowy Wierch became the main site for competitions. More than a century later, having organized the FIS World Championships three times (in 1929, 1939, and 1962), the Winter Universiade three times (in 1956, 1993, and 2001) and in recent years been a candidate city to host the Winter Olympics, it offers the most challenging terrain in Poland, with outstanding slopes and arguably the most stunning vistas of the Tatras.

Your day begins on the Kasprowy Wierch cable car, which was built, largely by hand, between 1935 and 1936 with up to 600 workers employed. So although you may face a long queue to ascend, you should treat it with due reverence (and to minimize your queuing, which can take as long as three hours, arrive early—it opens at 7.30 a.m. on

peak dates). The ascent to the top of Mount Kasprowy (6,517ft/1,987m above sea level) takes around ten minutes and takes place in two stages, with a change in Myślenickie Turnie 4,346ft (1,325m) up.

From the top there's a choice of two great slopes: Gasienicowa, a 0.9-mile- (1.4-km-) long black served by a modern quad chairlift; and our selected run, the longer Goryczkowa descent that drops 1,968 vertical feet (600m) over its 1.2-mile (2-km) length and takes a full 15 minutes to get back up on the aged double chairlift. Marvelous—plenty of thinking time.

The purist's choice

Most of the run is on open but steep-sided slopes for perfect, old-school, classic cruising, before the lower section hits the treeline shortly before the base of the chairlift. There are runs continuing down back to the base of the cable car (and the queue to get back up), but snow cover at lower elevations can be problematic. Being national parkland there's no snowmaking allowed, which should again please purists, but it does mean that there can be snow-cover issues. For the 2001 Winter Universiade this led to locals, aided by the Polish Army, diligently carting in truckloads of

LEFT: The slopes of Zakopane provide all levels of challenge, from beginner to expert.
RIGHT: The Kasprowy Wierch cable car is used not just by skiers and snowboarders but also by winter hikers, for whom a good, clear signpost is essential to set off on the right course rather than off down the steep piste.

snow to coat the brown slopes with a ribbon of snow when the natural stuff failed to arrive. This is unpredictable skiing as it used to be, but should snow cover be an issue, one of Zakopane's numerous other small ski areas (several have snowmaking) is usually open when Kasprowy Wierch is not.

Although scenically beautiful, the Tatra Mountains, the highest part of the Carpathian chain that stretches for more than 620 miles (1,000 km), are themselves only just over 31 miles (50km) long, peaking with Mount Gerlach (8,705ft/2,654m high). The local mountain marks the border between Poland and the Slovak Republic, which is not patroled by border guards and crossing is freely permitted. However, off-piste skiing is not permitted in the Tatra National Park, and park guards may fine transgressors. There's also an ever-present avalanche danger.

In touch with the female side

Today's great female skier Lyndsey Vonn should be interested in Zakopane, because it allowed women to compete in the Alpine Skiing World Championships staged here in 1929. Ms. Vonn, who has won pretty much everything there is to win in world skiing, put in a request to the International Ski Federation in 2012, which was subsequently

turned down, to be allowed to race with the men. But Ms. Vonn was not the first lady to do so, and in 1929 in Zakopane two women did compete. Adopting the "British rules," the Polish Ski Association invited "all comers" to the Championships and Doreen Elliott and Audrey Sale-Barker turned up from England, delighting the crowds by finishing 13th and 14th, beating 45 men who finished behind them.

Zakopane is also of interest to female ski racers because the 1939 Championships were, ironically but perhaps inevitably, dominated by German competitors, winning five of the six available titles shortly before the two countries went to war. These included a clean sweep of the ladies competition by Christl Cranz, who remains to this day the most successful downhill skier with 12 world championship golds.

Zakopane also has a major international reputation as a center for cross-country skiing, ski jumping, and biathlon. If you need one final reason to ski here, then the Polish Pope John Paul II, a keen skier now being made a saint by the Vatican (and in the process transforming his old ski kit into official Grade Two Holy Relics), officially blessed the slopes when he visited here. If that doesn't elevate Zakopane's skiing to among the world's best, then I don't know what could.

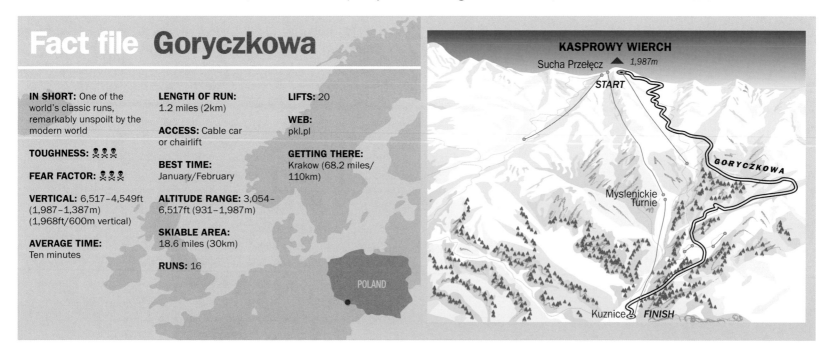

Fact file Goryczkowa

IN SHORT: One of the world's classic runs, remarkably unspoilt by the modern world

TOUGHNESS: ☠☠☠

FEAR FACTOR: ☠☠☠

VERTICAL: 6,517–4,549ft (1,987–1,387m) (1,968ft/600m vertical)

AVERAGE TIME: Ten minutes

LENGTH OF RUN: 1.2 miles (2km)

ACCESS: Cable car or chairlift

BEST TIME: January/February

ALTITUDE RANGE: 3,054–6,517ft (931–1,987m)

SKIABLE AREA: 18.6 miles (30km)

RUNS: 16

LIFTS: 20

WEB: pkl.pl

GETTING THERE: Krakow (68.2 miles/110km)

POLAND

KASPROWY WIERCH
Sucha Przełęcz ▲ 1,987m
START
GORYCZKOWA
Myslenickie Turnie
Kuznice *FINISH*

Itinerary 19
Palandöken, Turkey
10,417ft (3,176m)

Turkey is not on the radar of many skiers or boarders, but it deserves to be. With more than 90 mountain peaks topping 9,840ft (3,000m) and the highest, Ararat, at 16,849ft (5,137m), there's no shortage of terrain.

One of the "Westernizing" acts of its founder, Kemal Ataturk, was to sign Turkey up for International Ski Federation membership more than 70 years ago. Government interest in winter sports continues to this day, with the recent announcement of plans to build 50 ski areas to help boost the regional economy. So far around 30 ski areas have been created, one of the oldest, largest and closest to Istanbul (86.8 miles/140km away) being Uludag, also the best known. But with large, modern ski areas designed by international experts seeming to appear every year, entirely new terrain is being opened up, although Uludag has fought back by building one of the world's longest gondolas to link the resort to the slopes much more efficiently than in the past. One of the latest new arrivals is Mount Erciyes, which opened in 2012 with a 3,936-ft (1,200-m) vertical peaking at a year-round, 9,840-ft- (3,000-m-) high snow field and served by eight state-of-the-art lifts, mostly four- and six-seater chairlifts and a gondola—not the traditional image of skiing in Turkey.

A key stop on the Silk Road

However, the biggest success story in Turkish skiing over the past decade or so is the ancient city of Erzurum in Anatolia, located some 744 miles (1,200km) east of capital Ankara and 613.8 miles (990km) from Istanbul, a 90-minute flight away, but only a few hundred miles from the borders of Syria, Iran, Iraq, and Armenia. The 6,000-year-old settlement, once a key stop on the Silk Road, has spent various periods of its history being ruled over by one civilization after another (Hittites, Armenians, Mongols, Russians, Ottomans, Romans ...) and is ringed by high mountains, giving it the feel of somewhere like Innsbruck.

Although there were no real ski areas here at all little more than 15 years ago, more than US $300 million have been invested in transforming Erzurum into a ski resort, although you could still visit the city and not really be aware of it. First, there was the creation of Mount Palandöken in the late 1990s; but more recently, the new resort of Konakli and the Nordic center of Kandilli have transformed this university city with a third of a million inhabitants into a classic ski town, albeit without many of the locals really noticing. In 2011 it was chosen to host the Universiade Winter Games, attracting nearly 2,000 athletes from 58 nations.

But although Konakli, which lies 10.5 miles (17km) southwest of the city, was created to host Alpine racing for the Universiade, Mount Palandöken, 4.3 miles (7km) south of the city, remains the "must-ski" destination at Erzurum.

LEFT: Having existed without a ski slope nearby for all but the last decade or so of its 6,000-year history, the ancient city of Erzurum is perhaps a rather unlikely ski town.

RIGHT: Palandöken is one of the world's newest ski resorts but has quickly built its international reputation, including playing host to the Winter Universiade.

are an irresistible magnet to adventurous skiers

and boarders.

Why? Well, the mountain has the altitude to provide some of the longest runs in Turkey, and the snow cover and quality, too. Thanks to its altitude, north-facing location, and distance from the nearest sea, the same effect is at play as for Utah or Niseko: the moisture gets dried as it heads across the plains before dropping as light, fluffy powder on the slopes of Palandöken, normally building a base several feet deep by early February, with overnight foot-deep accumulations also the norm.

So far, so good. With few expert skiers in Turkey to appreciate this God-given gift, most of the groomed runs are not terribly inspiring, although you can enjoy gentle descents up to 6.2 miles (10km) long (this Ejder run is Turkey's longest). However, the vaguely conically shaped peaks are free of trees and many other major hazards, meaning that heading off into that powder is feasible if there's no avalanche danger; on the downside, it also means that the top of the mountain is quite wind exposed and windchill can be a significant factor. There are also reports of zealous liftees confiscating the passes of anyone heading off-piste without sticking to the itinerary routes and without seeking permission in advance.

To access the best runs you need to get above 8,200ft (2,500m), so take the Ejder chairlift to the area's highest point, from where you can survey a spectacular vista of the Kaçkar Mountains and Erzurum far below. Well, that's as long as it's not foggy, which is a common morning problem; less so by 11 a.m.

The off-piste itinerary route number 19, one of four marked on the piste map (you can make up many others yourself if you're careful), drops off the top of the chairlift and, if the snow is good, fullfils the "steep and deep" criteria most commonly required for a great ski run. Basically this is one wide-open powder bowl, and all you need to do is point your skis and shoot down. Yours are likely to be one of the few, if not the only, tracks in the snow, which is a big part of the pleasure of it.

To fully immerse yourself in the Turkish ski experience, the *après ski* meal has to be the famed *cağ* kebab of Erzurum (vegetarians should look away now). This is marinated leg of lamb roasted horizontally over an open wood fire, served on skewers with walnut-stuffed shredded wheat rolls and washed down with the local tea, which is drunk *kitlama*-style. It's actually best to leave the tea until after the kebab, because *kitlama*-style involves putting a big lump of sugar in your mouth and letting the tea gradually dissolve it with each sip. Don't tell your dentist. But with that meaty, nutty meal plus the sugar rush, you'll be in great shape to hit the powder again.

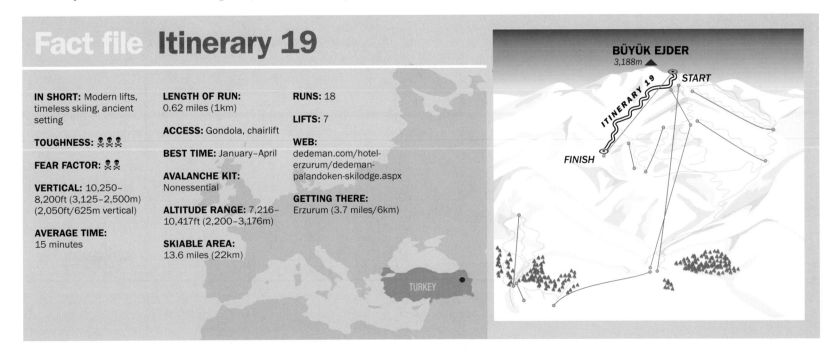

Fact file Itinerary 19

IN SHORT: Modern lifts, timeless skiing, ancient setting

TOUGHNESS: ☠☠☠

FEAR FACTOR: ☠☠

VERTICAL: 10,250–8,200ft (3,125–2,500m) (2,050ft/625m vertical)

AVERAGE TIME: 15 minutes

LENGTH OF RUN: 0.62 miles (1km)

ACCESS: Gondola, chairlift

BEST TIME: January–April

AVALANCHE KIT: Nonessential

ALTITUDE RANGE: 7,216–10,417ft (2,200–3,176m)

SKIABLE AREA: 13.6 miles (22km)

RUNS: 18

LIFTS: 7

WEB: dedeman.com/hotel-erzurum/dedeman-palandoken-skilodge.aspx

GETTING THERE: Erzurum (3.7 miles/6km)

TURKEY

BÜYÜK EJDER
3,188m ▲

ITINERARY 19

START

FINISH

Olympic Downhill
Sochi, Russia
7,498ft (2,286m)

Of the 50 runs in this book, 49 are, on the whole, long established. In some cases they have been skied for a century or more, building their reputations.

But great ski runs are still being created, and in a nod to the way the focus of ski-resort development has been moving in recent decades—essentially eastward, with most new resort development on Europe's Asian border or, indeed, in Asia itself—it seems only right to include the pretty new Olympic downhill course for the 2014 Sochi Winter Games.

The run was first unveiled to the world's fastest skiers in February 2012 and it met with almost universal approval. The run is "magnificent," according to Didier Cuche, while Aksel Lund Svindal, another of the greatest skiers of the modern era, describes the run as "what downhill is all about."

The Olympic downhill course is located at Rosa Khutor, created from scratch in 2003, and one of the four ski areas that have been developed around the resort town of Krasnaya Polyana, which itself is linked to the Black Sea resort of Sochi by a brand new road and rail service. Countless (and indeed unpublished) billions in almost any currency you choose to use were invested in these resorts—one of the few Russian media reports to give a figure went for "upward of US $30 billion," while the most excited talk of the overall project, with roads and rail through newly created mountain tunnels and a plethora of luxurious new hotels and an airport, added up to a nice round "$100 billion."

A technological revolution

In less than a decade this has changed the area from either empty mountainside or small rudimentary ski hills to, collectively, one of the largest and most technologically advanced ski regions on the planet. Around 50 lifts have been built, most of them high-speed, high-capacity chairlifts and gondolas—including the world's longest (17,656ft/5,383m) and, separately, biggest yet, capable of carrying cars in its cabins if access roads are blocked by snow.

Besides Rosa Khutor, the venue for the skiing speed events, the other ski areas here are Laura/Psekhako—the venue for most Nordic events—and the Alpika and Karusell ski areas. Together the four offer nearly 124 miles (200km) of terrain and the access lifts to three of them more or less interconnect.

These piste lengths and particularly combined uplift stats put Sochi straight up there in the top 20 of the world's biggest regions, including

BELOW: The most talked-about and the most expensive new piste of the 21st century was designed to host the world's best at the 2014 Sochi Winter Olympics. The longest Olympic downhill course ever built, at nearly 2.2 miles (3.5km), was designed by former racer Bernard Russi, the creator of most Olympic downhill courses of the past few decades. The young Austrian racer Matthias Mayer won the Olympic downhill on February 9, 2014, to the surprise of some. But Mayer does come from the neighboring village of Bad Kleinkirchheim, the home of another racing great, Franz Klammer, so perhaps they shouldn't be.

" IT COMBINES SPEED, TECHNIQUE AND A GRUELING VERTICAL DROP OF MORE THAN 3,280FT (1,000M), AS WELL AS SOME OF THE LONGEST JUMPS IN THE WORLD CUP. **"**

LEFT: The remarkable ski resort construction project at Sochi has created one of the world's biggest and best-equipped ski regions, almost from scratch, in less than ten years.
RIGHT: 31 miles (50km) up from the Black Sea and the buzz of Sochi, the Rosa Khutor Alpine Resort is part of the Olympic village and hosted the Alpine skiing events for the 2014 Winter Olympics and Paralympics.

the Arlberg, Zillertal 3000, and Skiwelt in Austria; Espace Killy or La Plagne in France; Italy's Milky Way or Val Gardena; and Grandvalira in Andorra. No other areas in the world quite measure up in terms of the number of high-spec lifts, either.

It's all pretty impressive considering there were just a couple of old double chairlifts in the region a decade ago. The only downside appears to be bureaucracy. While in western Europe and North America these days you may be scanned as you pass through a lift station so that you can get a computer measurement of your day's skiing to post on Facebook, the lift scanners at Sochi are metal detectors to deter terrorists.

One of the toughest on the Olympic circuit

The men's downhill course at Rosa Khutor itself is one of the longest ever built at just under 2.2 miles (3.5km) and has rapidly gained a reputation as one of the toughest on the circuit, even before hosting the Olympics. It combines speed, technique and a grueling vertical drop of more than 3,280ft (1,000m), as well as some of the longest jumps in the World Cup. The course was designed by former racer Bernard Russi,

who also designed the famed Birds of Prey downhill course at Beaver Creek, along with many other famous runs.

Accessed by the area's top gondola, with a ski down through avalanche-prone terrain high above the treeline to the top of the run, it carves its way down around the contours of the mountain. Distinguishing features for racers tackling it at top speed include multiple tight turns, which can be hard to make, and five long jumps spaced throughout the course. With many turns and few gliding sections there are limited opportunities for racers to get into a tuck position, and the first 40 seconds or so of the run is perhaps reminiscent more of a super-G than a downhill, albeit a very fast one with a series of technical steep, narrow turns. The middle section contains some quirky bumps and rolls to negotiate, then toward the end the course eases out, although there's a final big jump close to the finish.

If you decide not to take the downhill course every time, then the top gondola also provides access to freeride terrain for which the original ski area at Krasnaya Polyana was famed for decades before the region won the right to stage the Olympics, with generally high scores for the steep terrain and quality of the powder. You can also enjoy great views to the Black Sea from the top of the mountain.

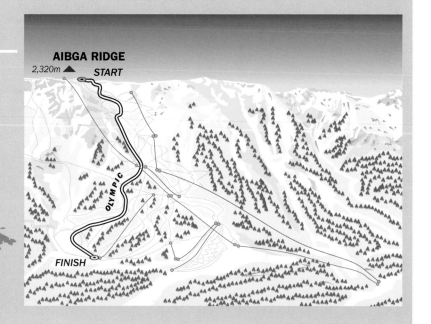

Fact file **Olympic Downhill**

IN SHORT: The world's newest Olympic course is set to become a classic

TOUGHNESS:
☠☠☠

FEAR FACTOR: ☠☠☠

VERTICAL: 6,708–3,083ft (2,045–940m) (3,559ft/1,085m vertical)

AVERAGE TIME: Three minutes

LENGTH OF RUN: 2.16 miles (3.49km)

ACCESS: Gondola

BEST TIME: December–April

AVALANCHE KIT: Nonessential

ALTITUDE RANGE: 2,686–7,498ft (819–2,286m)

SKIABLE AREA: 44.6 miles (72km) (Sochi

Region 119 miles/192km)

RUNS: 20 (Sochi Region 65)

LIFTS: 15 (Sochi Region 51)

WEB: rosaski.com

GETTING THERE: Adler International Airport (27.9 miles/45km)

RUSSIA

AIBGA RIDGE
2,320m ▲ START
OLYMPIC
FINISH

Asia

Southeast Shoulder to Drang
Gulmarg, India
13,031ft (3,979m)

Gulmarg—which, unhelpfully for a ski resort means "meadow of flowers"—has a colorful and sometimes bloody history. Originally a retreat of regional kings, it was established as a mountain station by British colonials in the 19th century and then used to stage skiing competitions from 1927 up to the Second World War. In the modern era, attempts to develop the resort to its world-class potential were thwarted through much of the late 20th century thanks to its location in Kashmir, on land disputed by India and Pakistan (it's 95 percent Muslim), leading to militarization of the area and the occasional attack by terrorists/separatists (depending on your point of view).

Although the military presence remains prominent, things have been much calmer since the start of this century (or at least they are as I write and hopefully still will be as you read). New lifts and a (very) long-planned, French-built gondola, which finally fully opened in 2005 after more than a decade "under construction" and rises from 9,742 to 13,054ft (2,970–3,980m) above sea level, have been installed. Gulmarg is a year-round beauty spot that frequently appears in Bollywood movies and claims to be home to the world's highest golf course, once all that snow has melted away.

With the exception of the Jade Dragon slopes in China's Yunnan province, there is currently no higher ski resort operating in the world.

You really do have to get used to the altitude, probably with a couple of days spent lower down to acclimatize your body. The Gulmarg gondola tops out at just 13,120ft (4,000m), just below the summit of Mount Apharwat at 13,527ft (4,124m).

The skiable area is almost unlimited, boasting verticals of over 4,920ft (1,500m), big powder bowls, chutes, cornice jumps, and cruising through ancient pine woods as some of the highlights you can expect. And these are just the ski attractions. Add to that an exotic mix of local shrines, villages, and the incredible Kashmiri cuisine and you know for sure you're not in a standard ski resort replicated the world over.

46ft (14m) of powder

Gulmarg is best suited to advanced and expert skiers and boarders. You should be happy to go off-piste most of the time and cope with potential altitude sickness well enough to not let that put you off.

Gulmarg's skiing itself is something very different. Consider that most users of the gondola are sightseers, that there are few advanced-level skiers here (and quite a few of them will be using the heliski service that promises even bigger 6,560-ft/2,000-m verticals) and that there is a divide between novices and powderhounds that have flown in from around the world. Thus the groomed and patroled terrain is very limited and targeted primarily at first-timers.

The rest of the 3.1-mile- (5-km-) wide slopes of Mount Apharwat is simply wide-open mountain face with a vast variety of terrain, including some spectacular steeps combined with remarkable deeps ... of powder. In fact, Gulmarg's annual snowfall is, like all Gulmarg measurements, slightly vague and prone to exaggeration, but claims of up to 46ft (14m) falling through a good season are not unrealistic and put Gulmarg up there with Niseko (Japan) and Mount Baker (Washington State, USA) as the top three recipients of the most snow in the world.

LEFT: Even though the ridge itself looks modest in comparison to surrounding peaks, Gulmarg gets some of the heaviest snowfalls in the area and has rightly earned itself the moniker "best ski resort in the Himalayas."
RIGHT: Thanks to the gondola that was installed in 2005 and ascends to almost 13,120ft (4,000m) above sea level, Gulmarg is one of the highest lift-served resorts in the world.

RIGHT: The top of the Gulmarg ridge affords some spectacular views of the surrounding Himalayan peaks, something only a select few ski resorts in the world can offer.

BELOW: Even through there aren't any fancy chalets where you might be served *jäger* tea or a cappuccino, there are some great spots in the hill-village of Gulmarg to sample the famous Kashmiri cuisine.

The lack of serious skiers on Gulmarg's slopes makes it possible to ski laps through the powder using the queue-free gondola to return to the top of the slopes, with the most zealous early starters typically getting in at least ten descents and more than 32,800ft (10,000m) of vertical through the powder within a day.

As with a few other areas described in this book where the options are fairly limited (one thinks particularly of Greenland, Nepal, or even Las Leñas), choosing the run for Gulmarg is tricky. A vast selection of bowls, chutes, and gullies are immediately apparent below as you ascend the upper section of the two-stage gondola from the Kongdori mid-station at 10,112ft (3,083m) above sea level, with few people to ski them. Hike a little higher from the top and you can not only enjoy views of K2 on a clear day, but also gain access to still steeper descents, jumping off ridges and through cornices into extreme bowls. There's also excellent tree skiing down beneath massive pines, particularly to the Tangmarg valley below, and even a kind of mogul run, known lovingly as Mughuls, alongside popular trails such as Shark Fins, G-4, Beta, Gujjar Hut, and Sunshine Peak.

A grim reputation for avalanches

Perhaps most revered are the runs down from Apharwat's southeast shoulder, accessed directly from the gondola, that allow you to ski on down for more than 5,576 vertical feet (1,700m) past Gulmarg itself to the valley floor near Drang. It is serious off-piste terrain that should not be attempted without a guide.

Partly due to its sensational snowfall reputation and steep terrain, Gulmarg has a grim reputation for avalanches, so it is always wise to play it safe and find low-angle terrain beyond the avalanche-prone areas if conditions are questionable. Most avalanches occur outwith the ski-area boundary (one in the region infamously killed 17 Indian army soldiers in training in February 2010), but some also happen in-bounds, with guided groups not immune.

But to end on a positive, although the British are long gone from here and you're more likely to run into Australian or French skiers or boarders, the service remains "Raj style" and the value high, while your ski experience is made all the more unique by the sights, colors, and aromas of skiing in India. And foreign tourists may not have Gulmarg's steeper terrain to themselves for long. Local people, along with the *nouveau riche* of India's billion-plus population, are clamoring to take to the slopes too, with ski courses invariably oversubscribed and all available equipment rented out.

In any case, the growing number of fans of Gulmarg, both local and international, will tell you that if you arrive when conditions are perfect and neither the weather nor the local bureaucracy has closed that upper stage of the gondola, there's no better skiing to be had.

Fact file Southeast Shoulder to Drang

IN SHORT: Wide-open skiing on the world's highest big-powder vertical

TOUGHNESS: ☠☠☠☠

FEAR FACTOR: ☠☠☠☠

VERTICAL: 13,054–7,380ft (3,980–2,250m) (5,674ft/1,730m vertical)

AVERAGE TIME: Two hours

LENGTH OF RUN: 3.7 miles (6km)

ACCESS: Gondola

BEST TIME: January–May

AVALANCHE KIT: Essential

ALTITUDE RANGE: 8,954–13,051ft (2,730–3,979m)

SKIABLE AREA: 43.4 miles (70km)

RUNS: 33

LIFTS: 6

WEB: skihimalaya.com

GETTING THERE: Srinagar (34.7 miles/56km)

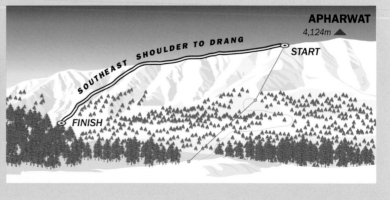

INDIA

APHARWAT
4,124m ▲

SOUTHEAST SHOULDER TO DRANG

START

FINISH

Fishtail Base Camp Run
Annapurna Sanctuary, Nepal
17,056ft (5,200m)

Despite being home to the world's highest mountains, some of the greatest vertical descents, spectacular Himalayan scenery and some of the planet's best snow for skiing, Nepal remained off-limits to skiers right through the 20th century as the sport spread from a few small, pioneering centers right around the world.

From the late 1970s onward, some extreme skiers and boarders had gained permission to climb above 26,240ft (8,000m) in the Nepalese Himalayas to descend the slopes of Manaslu, Annapurna, Cho Oyu, Dhaulagiri, and Everest itself, but for those who were not extreme skiers as well as skilled highest-altitude mountaineers, Nepal was out of bounds.

That finally changed in 2001 when, after three years of planning and consultation, a company called Himalayan Heliski Guides finally gained permission to open up Nepal to heliskiers. The agreement with the Nepalese government ensured that all the areas skied would be done so with respect for the local Nepalese people, their traditions, wildlife, and the environment.

Begin with an early-morning helidrop

From that first winter of 2000–01 onward the company's clients have made numerous first descents, creating the ski map of Nepal in the process and having the honor of naming the runs they ski first. The company has now been operating for more than a dozen seasons, offering tours when conditions are at their best in the late winter and early spring each year, and has therefore built up a great deal of experience and quite a detailed map, having heliskied in the Everest, Annapurna, Dhaulagiri, and Humla regions of Nepal. So which is best?

"There are so many great runs, it's very hard to choose—all of them are unique in their own way," says company boss Craig Calonica. "But if I have to choose, it's a run in the Annapurna Sanctuary that we didn't ski until our seventh season in 2007 that is the very best—the most spectacular run in all of Nepal," he continues. Craig was one of the world's top ten ski racers from the mid-1970s to the late 1980s and has skied all over the world, including more than 30 years in the Himalayas.

"The terrain, snow conditions, and views are something that skiers' and boarders' dreams are made of," Craig asserts, and his experience of Nepalese snow conditions is unmatched, having been skiing in the country since 1981. This includes several attempts to ski down Everest, during one of which, in 1998, he had the idea of starting a heliskiing operation.

The run begins with an early-morning helidrop at 16,728ft (5,100m) to take advantage of the unique microclimate of the southern Annapurna region. This 69.4-mile- (112-km-) long, north-facing

You will be completely on your own as you glide down the massive slopes in the Annapurna Sanctuary, with scenery that you won't find anywhere else in the world.

RIGHT: Fishtail Peak looms in the background above the town of Pokhara, one of the most popular tourist destinations in Nepal, with three of the world's highest mountains—Dhaulagiri, Annapurna I, and Manaslu—within close proximity to the city.

FAR RIGHT: With the incredible altitudes you reach when heliskiing in the Annapurna region, the thin and unpolluted air makes the normally blue sky appear almost black, even at midday.

mountain chain is one of the most westerly in Nepal, which puts it in the best position to benefit from prevailing weather conditions and get the best of the snow-bearing clouds first. Indeed, the area is well known for getting late-afternoon thunder showers that frequently leave fresh boot-top to knee-deep powder the next morning with blue skies. "It's as close to having a powder-making machine as it gets," says Craig.

To make the most of these unusual conditions, the company starts early and finishes early, still fitting in the equivalent of a full day's heliskiing, but flying out from their base at Pokhara to the top of the run at 6.30 a.m. and skiing until the clouds start to roll in, which can be any time from 11 a.m. to 12 noon.

Once you set off, the first section is a big, wide-open area with perfect terrain for skiing or boarding. Take your pick between any kind of turn you like here, be it big open turns or small linked turns; it's your choice.

About halfway down the pitch of the run, things begin to get a bit steeper. Here there's also a choice when you go to your left over a small ridge, from where you can either ski a challenging couloir next to the wall that forms the ridge, or go a bit further still to the left where the terrain is more open. Either line is excellent, and the terrain is perfect.

Welcoming smiles and a cup of tea

The run resumes its regular flow and continues right on down the valley to end at Fishtail Lodge, which sits 4,592 vertical feet (1,400m) below the drop point at 12,136ft (3,700m). Here the Nepalese operating the lodge are waiting for you with welcoming smiles and cups of tea.

Each group of four to eight skiers contains at least two internationally qualified guides who descend at the front and back of the group, ensuring that the route is safe and the party stays together. The first descent was made in 2007 by Craig and his friends Stephane Dan, Karine Ruby, and Fred Mathieu, who had it all to themselves.

Along with the joy of the run itself throughout the descent, and while heliskiing neighboring runs in this region, there are always spectacular views of the south face of Annapurna I and Machapuchare—also known as Fishtail Peak. Surrounding these two well-known peaks are several lesser-known mountains that complement the beauty of this area, ensuring it lives up to its reputation for being one of the most visually stunning regions in Nepal's Himalaya.

Take in a Buddhist temple

The skiing day is over by lunchtime, when the helicopter flies out before the snow-bearing clouds close off the valley, depositing the powder ready for the next morning's trip. After what will hopefully have been the greatest ski day of your life, lunch is enjoyed in Pokhara, a lakeside town popularly regarded as one of Nepal's nicest, where you can also look up at the Annapurnas where you spent the morning before spending the afternoon, if you have the energy, enjoying some of the other sports in the region (biking, golf) or perhaps taking in a little of the local culture at a Buddhist temple, for example.

The best time to ski the run is from mid-February, and heliskiing continues through to April. The winter snows come late in Nepal compared to most skiing nations, and in most years do not arrive until late January or early February.

Of course, you do not travel all the way to Annapurna just to do the one run, however much worthy of the effort that one run may be. On average you will ski four to six runs a day, from Monday through Friday, and have Saturday for a makeup day if needed. Himalayan Heliski Guides are based in Pokhara the entire week, from where you can make plenty of other heliski excursions.

The Annapurna descents

One of the most popular adventures is to travel a little further to heliski in the Annapurna north region for the day. It's a longer flight from Pokhara, so take-off is at six in the morning. Typically it's possible to get in four to six runs before returning back to Pokhara after the ski day is done.

The north side of the Annapurna is once again a spectacular area, with great views of Annapurna II, III, and IV. The terrain is excellent, the drops higher, the vertical descents even bigger, and the runs even longer than on the south side, although Craig still rates that run on the south as slightly closer to perfection for the complete package of scenery, skiing, and snow.

Heliskiing or heliboarding on both the north and south side of the Annapurna is a great experience, and one that every serious skier should try at least once in their skiing career. Doing both is well worth the extra flying time.

Fact file Fishtail Base Camp

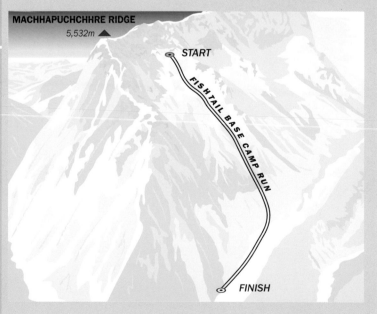

MACHHAPUCHCHHRE RIDGE
5,532m ▲

START

FISHTAIL BASE CAMP RUN

FINISH

IN SHORT: Like dying and going to ski heaven

TOUGHNESS:
☠☠☠ ('The altitude is a bit tough the first two days')

FEAR FACTOR:
☠ ('No fear, just pure pleasure')

VERTICAL: 16,728–12,136ft (5,100–3,700m) (4,592ft/1,400m vertical)

AVERAGE TIME: Approx. 30 minutes, dictated

by skiers' ability and group size

LENGTH OF RUN: 3.1 miles (5km)

ACCESS: Helicopter

BEST TIME: February–April

AVALANCHE KIT: Essential

ALTITUDE RANGE: 17,056–12,136ft (5,200–3,700m)

SKIABLE AREA: Unlimited

RUNS: Unlimited

LIFTS: 0 (heli only)
WEB: heliskinepal.com
GETTING THERE: Tribhuvan International Airport, Kathmandu (purchase tourist visa on arrival). Domestic flight from Kathmandu to Pokhara where HHSG are based (25-min flight). Helicopter flight to Annapurna Sanctuary from Pokhara, 15 mins. 25-min flight into the Annapurna north region.

NEPAL

Mizuno no Sawa
Niseko, Japan
4,290ft (1,308m)

The first time I skied Niseko, I met a mixed group of well-heeled, powder-obsessed skiers and boarders from Sweden who had spent two decades (and presumably a considerable amount of money) "checking out" ski areas around the world with a reputation for deep powder. Not just deep, either, but weightless, light, fluffy stuff. They told me that their quest was complete. Five seasons earlier they had arrived in Niseko and stopped searching: the snow here is the best on the planet, they said.

I have to agree. Niseko's snow is the best for quality and quantity combined. The air dries as it crosses the thousands of miles of plains that cover the eastern Asian mainland. That air then hits the Sea of Japan, where it sucks up moisture, then rises rapidly as it bounces into the western flanks of the mountains of Hokkaido, Japan's most northerly major island. Here it dumps vast volumes of light powder. Niseko's average annual tally of 52ft (16m) is not quite the world's biggest (a title held by Mount Baker in Washington State, USA, a resort almost directly due east on the same latitude as Niseko, with 62ft/19m) but purists rate Niseko's snow as, usually, better.

Not only is there the powder, there's also the mountain. Mount Yōtei —6,225ft (1,898m)—dominates the view from the slopes: a visually perfect (and still active) volcano that appears to be a scale replica of Mount Fuji. It hasn't erupted in 3,000 years, but the geothermal activity helps to supply hot water for the various *onsen* (hot-water springs) in the area—the perfect natural *après-ski* hot tubs.

The Japanese themselves are less enthralled by all the snow and clear it away efficiently from roads, roofs, lifts, and pistes; skiing on it in its uncompressed state has not, historically, been the norm. During the boom years of Japanese skiing in the 1980s, the groomed pistes were filled from dawn until late at night with determined skiers, but off-piste was against most resorts' rules (minimum penalty: lift pass confiscation). Those resorts that did allow it usually required that you register with the local police station before heading out of bounds.

Exploring Mizuno no Sawa

A decade or so later, the Australians arrived. Finding ski areas in a country that was going through harder economic times but in a similar time zone to back home, they sensed business opportunities. Aussies

" ... THEY HAD ARRIVED IN NISEKO AND STOPPED SEARCHING: THE SNOW HERE IS THE BEST ON THE PLANET, THEY SAID. "

arrived in droves, to Niseko in particular, quickly overcoming the language barrier and altering the ski area's mindset so that gates started opening onto the backcountry and all that untouched powder. But although powderhounds from around the world began arriving in greater numbers, excited by the powder, there were complaints about the terrain. These were essentially, "it's too tame."

Niseko's answer is Mizuno no Sawa, a once "permanently off-limits" bowl beneath the Niseko gondola in the Higashiyama sector of the resort. It had long been seen as an attraction by backcountry skiers, but the avalanche danger was high and three fatalities had been reported among those who did not obey the warnings. Niseko brought in local and international avalanche experts in 2008 to try something largely unheard of in the country—setting off avalanches manually to clear the danger and open the area to skiers and boarders.

The plan worked, the Japanese government was convinced, and it's now possible to ski this bowl and some of the steepest lift-accessed powder fields in Japan (lift access is useful in a land where hiking up can result in sinking up to your neck in snow and having to "swim" out).

However, it's not quite as simple as just turning up ready to ski the bowl, accessed from the top of the Speedy Wonder lift. You must normally preregister your interest at least the day before you plan to go for it, and attend a ten minute safety lecture (small fee payable) before you can enter the bowl in the company of a ski patrol. You should be an expert skier or boarder, aged over 16, and carry an avalanche transceiver. There are normally two descents a day (one first thing in the morning, and the second descent around lunchtime), with a maximum of 50 people in each group.

Permission to ski the bowl has been hard won and Haru no Taki, the strictly off-limits area next to Mizuno no Sawa with high avalanche danger, remains permanently closed. If any participants in the program duck under the ropes in order to access the closed-off areas, the whole operation in Mizuno no Sawa will be stopped.

Head up to the "wild north" of Japan, attend that prerun lecture, and resist the temptation to ski into unnecessary danger. Your reward will be incredibly deep powder in some of the steepest bowl skiing in Japan, and the effort that brought you there in the first place will all be worth it.

Fact file Mizuno no Sawa

IN SHORT: Some are steeper, (almost) none are deeper

TOUGHNESS: ☠☠☠

FEAR FACTOR: ☠☠☠

VERTICAL: 3,979–1,092ft (1,213–333m) (2,952ft/900m vertical)

AVERAGE TIME: 20 minutes

LENGTH OF RUN: 1.2 miles (2km)

ACCESS: Speedy Wonder lift with obligatory safety lecture beforehand

BEST TIME: December–March

AVALANCHE KIT: Essential

ALTITUDE RANGE: 984–4,290ft (300–1,308m)

SKIABLE AREA: 29.1 miles (47km)

RUNS: 34

LIFTS: 20

WEB: nisekotourism.com

GETTING THERE: Sapporo (68.2 miles/110km)

JAPAN

NISEKO AN'NUPURI
▲ 1,308m

START

MIZUNO NO SAWA

Annupuri

FINISH

Niseko village ski resort

Southern Hemisphere

Roca Jack
Portillo, Chile
10,857ft (3,310m)

A bit out of the way for most people, Portillo is nonetheless one of the world's top ski resorts, and has become a training ground for many of the world's top ski teams due to the reversal of seasons. The best time to visit is normally around July.

> **" THE ASCENT IS STEEP AND PRONE TO AVALANCHE, MEANING THAT ANY FIXED LIFT OF THE CONVENTIONAL SORT RISKED DAMAGE AND LONG PERIODS OF REPAIR. "**

Portillo is both a unique and iconic resort, located a couple of hours northeast of the Chilean capital Santiago and just a few miles from the Argentinian border in the high Andes. It has built a reputation as a "must-ski" resort for generations of skiers ever since it first came to global fame by hosting the World Alpine Ski Championships in 1966. The world's best ski racers still train here every summer on its challenging, exciting terrain.

In fact, the resort's roots as a ski area are among the world's oldest. It had first been skied nearly 130 years ago by Norwegian railroad surveyors, and when the Trans-Andean railroad was finally built in 1910, skiers used it to access the slopes of what was to become Portillo.

The famed Portillo powder

It was the Chilean government who first tried to market Portillo as a ski resort. They built the famous yellow hotel at its base and even hired the greatest skier of the time, the Frenchman Emile Allias, to run the ski school. Allias was a former world champion, and among many achievements in his 100 years of life, he developed several great ski resorts around the world. Eventually, in the mid-1950s, the government decided to sell the resort to an American called Bob Purcell, who then brought Portillo up to international resort standards. His family have run it ever since.

On the slopes, Portillo is famed for its advanced terrain and its powder skiing (heliskiing is a popular option) and it has a great sunshine record—four days in every five are sunny. It also still manages to clock up an average of 20ft (6m) of fresh snow a year. With a maximum of 450 guests in that famous yellow hotel, which maintains the community-style, all-inclusive experience it has offered since the 1950s, the resort is also known for having no lift queues and uncrowded slopes.

Despite all that powder, around 80 percent of Portillo's runs are groomed every night. These include the popular Plateau trail, the scene of Jean-Claude Killy's win in those 1966 World Championships two years before he swept the board at the Grenoble Winter Olympics (Franz Klammer was also there, and famously forgot to remove his ski boots, or his skis, before taking a dip in the hotel pool). But Roca Jack, arguably Portillo's most famous and most challenging marked trail, is one of the few marked runs left in its natural state.

Avalanche-prone lifts

Roca Jack has built up its fame over nearly 70 years. It was one of the first runs to be created at the resort, and still attracts the world's best teams for training each summer, with the Austrian, Canadian, Slovenian, and US teams being regular returnees.

Located on the Juncalillo side of Portillo's ski area, Roca Jack gets the sunshine early each day. This makes it the first run to soften in the morning sun, so it's a great run to ski first thing.

Along with its challenge, the run also offers spectacular views from top to bottom. A short hike past the top of the lift, you can see the peak of Aconcagua which, at 22,835ft (6,962m), is the tallest in both the western and southern hemispheres and one of the world's so-called "Seven Summits"— the highest peaks on each of the continents. Many other Andean peaks in the 19,680-ft (6,000-m) range are also visible, and as you descend the run you have a wonderful view of the Inca lake below, all the way from start to finish.

The run's history dates right back to the founding of Portillo in the 1940s. One of the earliest enthusiasts for the resort and its now-legendary terrain was an American called Jack Heaton, who spent several seasons there, skiing the old-fashioned way by walking up. In the spring Jack liked nothing more than to set out early and climb up to one of the peaks to the left of the lake, take in the view, and then, when the snow had warmed up a little and conditions were perfect, ski down. His favorite route became known as Roca Jack, now Portillo's most revered and famed descent.

Just to add to the run's reputation, as Portillo's popularity increased, so the need for a ski lift to access Roca Jack was increasingly discussed. The ascent is steep and prone to avalanche, meaning that any fixed lift of the conventional sort risked damage and long periods of repair. The great lift-designing mind of Jean Pomagalski, the original owner and boss of the famous POMA lift company, was given the challenge and he came up with the *Va et Vient* ("Come and Go") lift.

A kind of half-cable car, half-draglift, it has no towers but three bull wheels, one at the bottom of the slope and two at the top. Two tow bars with up to five platter-style button seats attached are connected to this contraption, pulling up to five skiers, side by side, quickly up the slope —an experience likened to uphill water skiing and part of the challenge and legend of Roca Jack.

LEFT: The vast and often very steep terrain of Roca Jack means that you are often completely on your own, and able to make fresh tracks even in the afternoon sun.

If the lift is damaged by an avalanche when the area is closed due to avalanche danger, it is designed to be released so that the cable can be buried without damaging the lift. That means that it can be repaired or, if necessary, replaced within a few days.

Views of the highest South American peak

Once you have skied Roca Jack a few times, you may wish to use the *Va et Vient* lift to access more runs in the area. Some of the other famous contenders, avalanche danger permitting, include the Super C Couloir, accessed via an out-of-bounds hike off Portillo's Roca Jack up to the summit and then down the slope that opens up into Portillo's El Estadio run. If you don't opt for the Super C, you can traverse across from the top of Roca Jack to ski down the speed-skiing course, Kilometro Lanzado ("Flying Kilometer"), where speed skiing was first pioneered in the early 1960s. The 124-mile (200-km) speed barrier was broken on skis here for the first time in 1978 by Steve McKinney.

The Super C Couloir is a legendary route at Portillo for only the most experienced skiers and it all starts on the Roca Jack *Va et Vient*. At the top of the lift, start climbing very steeply straight up to the summit—depending on the snow conditions, the hike can take from two to four hours. Once you've climbed up the narrow gorge of Roca Jack leading to the peak of Ojos de Agua, which can include exposed points in the climb, you will find amazing views of Aconcagua (22,835ft/6,962m), the highest mountain in the world outside the Himalayas. You can also see at least another 12 towering mountains over 19,680ft (6,000m), which will make you feel small in the immensity of the Andes. Absolute silence, peace, and an incredible view make it worth the effort to get there.

The return is through the Super C couloir itself, dropping down approximately 4,264ft (1,300m) and ending at El Estadio run, and from there to the base of the Juncalillo chair. It is recommended only for expert skiers with a very good level of skiing or snowboarding, fitness, and strength. Never go alone; always go with an experienced fellow skier and make sure you have the right equipment. You will want to bring a transceiver or pager (for avalanches), shovel, and probe, water to stay hydrated, and a snack to combat fatigue.

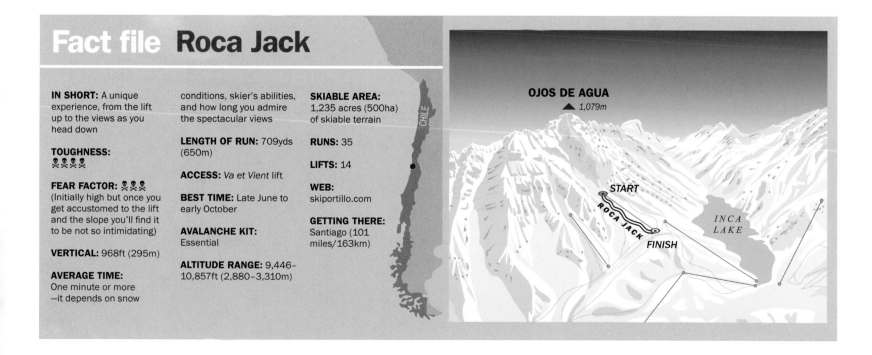

Fact file Roca Jack

IN SHORT: A unique experience, from the lift up to the views as you head down

TOUGHNESS:
☠☠☠☠

FEAR FACTOR: ☠☠☠ (Initially high but once you get accustomed to the lift and the slope you'll find it to be not so intimidating)

VERTICAL: 968ft (295m)

AVERAGE TIME: One minute or more —it depends on snow

conditions, skier's abilities, and how long you admire the spectacular views

LENGTH OF RUN: 709yds (650m)

ACCESS: *Va et Vient* lift

BEST TIME: Late June to early October

AVALANCHE KIT: Essential

ALTITUDE RANGE: 9,446– 10,857ft (2,880–3,310m)

SKIABLE AREA: 1,235 acres (500ha) of skiable terrain

RUNS: 35

LIFTS: 14

WEB: skiportillo.com

GETTING THERE: Santiago (101 miles/163km)

CHILE

OJOS DE AGUA
▲ 1,079m

START
ROCA JACK
FINISH

INCA LAKE

Eduardo's
Las Leñas, Argentina
11,250ft (3,430m)

Las Leñas opened just 30 years ago but, according to the excellent *South America Ski Guide* by Chris Lizza, published less than ten years after that, it had a colorful period prior to opening. This included billionaire owners in the 1970s commissioning Aspen staff to look at the possibilities of a ski area at the site, before those owners were kidnapped by apparently Robin Hood-like guerrillas who demanded a $60 millon ransom be paid out to the local poor. Legend has it (and it's a legend some dispute) that some truckloads of consumer goods were distributed and the then owners of Las Leñas were released after nine months, quickly deciding to sell up. Despite Aspen's report on the potential being less than glowing, according to Mr. Lizza, the next owners forged ahead, and eventually Las Leñas was born.

I don't know if Aspen's 1970s report highlighted the "issues" with Las Leñas that appear in all objective reviews of the resort since then, but they are as follows: wind—the resort has a reputation for exceptionally strong winds that close lifts; snow—there is sometimes too much falling at once in huge storms for operations to cope with, causing closures, or too little (only 28in/72cm fell all winter in 1985), and this "too little" problem is reported to have been an issue for several seasons recently for those who love their powder; terrain—limited easy terrain for a mainstream resort development; and finally lifts—the closure of them due to wind and snow can lead to long queues at those still open.

Las Leñas is as close as you can get to heliskiing without the use of a helicopter. You are dropped off by the Marte chairlift around the back before you make your way across the incredible line of Eduardo's, past these awesome rock spires.

LEFT: The Las Leñas hype is for real: the area boasts the longest sustained verticals in South America, with an average of 40 percent over 7,872ft (2,400m). The Eduardo couloir drops down between these infamous spires into the middle of the area near the Minerva chairlift.

None of these factors sound like great selling points for Las Leñas or provide a likely backdrop to one of the greatest runs in the world, I know, and I take this opportunity to apologize to the resort's marketing department.

A vast terrain for experts

To start tipping the balance back in favor of Las Leñas, I would first like to highlight the magnificent Andean scenery with which the area is blessed, with dramatic towering peaks of yellowish stone, slightly reminiscent of the Dolomites but on a still-larger scale, towering above and there to be skied between.

I would also invite you to think about the upside—namely, that when the snow is deep, the wind has dropped, and the upper lifts are running, then the other often-used description of the resort comes into play: "ski forever." Because Las Leñas is vast, often referred to as the biggest— when you count all of the off-piste opportunities—and has the largest resort footprint in both southern and western hemispheres.

While officially much of the resort's terrain best suits beginner and intermediate skiers and boarders, the actual percentage of terrain suited to experts is vast, when you can get to it. That's because most of the resort's more extreme, lift-accessible terrain is reached via the Marte chairlift, and when that closes much of it can't be reached.

Most of the people skiing off-piste are Europeans, North Americans, and their ilk, but it's important to keep in mind that this is Wild West terrain and so it's important to be fully avalanche aware, know your limits, and to ski with a local guide or other expert if you head into that limitless backcountry.

There's so much terrain, skied by comparatively so few people, that choosing the ultimate run here is one of those impossible tasks. In the backcountry you can pretty well create your own great run if you're prepared to hike up, although a sizable chunk can be accessed by a snowcat service.

So to provide some limit, even though Las Leñas itself may not, I'm going to stick in-bounds, ignore the delights of the Juno Bowl and El Collar and the supersteep Sin Nombre, and choose the same run that the organizers of the Freeskiing World Tour opted for when they rolled into town in 2010: Eduardo's.

One of an estimated 40 different chutes accessed from the high plateau, 11,152ft (3,400m) up at the top of the Marte chair, Eduardo's is very long, sweeping down for the best part of 3,280 vertical feet (1,000m) within a rocky gully. There are no trees at Las Leñas and Eduardo's is essentially one steep, long, rock garden—and hopefully, when you visit, a powder paradise where you carve turns through fluffy white stuff and bounce off snow-covered boulders.

You'll probably want to ski laps, even if the ride back up is likely to take you some 40 minutes, probably stopping to refuel at Santa Fe next to the all-important Marte chair thanks to its convenient location and normally excellent food.

Always remember to ski safely in this big country. Ideally bring your own transceiver and other avalanche safety gear with you, as they're not always easy to rent in the resort. Indeed, the issues of skiing this terrain are highlighted by the existence of chutes with exciting-sounding Spanish names such as Sin Salida, which is accessed from the Marte chair.

Ski into this and you'll most likely discover too late that Sin Salida is Spanish for "to a dead end"—which translates in physical terms to a steep hike back up or negotiating a 33-ft (10-m) cliff, so ski with a local guide.

Fact file Eduardo's

IN SHORT: When it's good, it's unbelievably good

TOUGHNESS: ☠☠☠☠

FEAR FACTOR: ☠☠☠☠

VERTICAL: 11,152–7,872ft (3,400-2,400m) (3,280ft/1,000m vertical)

AVERAGE TIME: 15 minutes

LENGTH OF RUN: 1.2 miles (2km)

ACCESS: Marte chairlift

BEST TIME: July–August

AVALANCHE KIT: Essential

ALTITUDE RANGE: 7,310-11,250ft (2,256–3,430m)

SKIABLE AREA: 24

RUNS: 40

LIFTS: 11

WEB: SouthAmericaSki.com LasLenasSki.com laslenas.com

GETTING THERE: Marlargue (49.6 miles/ 80km), then by ski bus or rental car

ARGENTINA

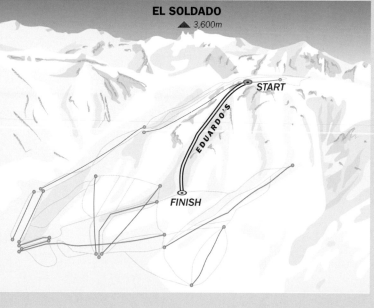

EL SOLDADO
▲ 3,600m

START

EDUARDO'S

FINISH

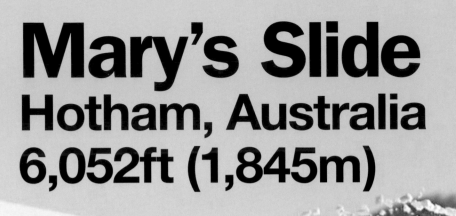

Mary's Slide
Hotham, Australia
6,052ft (1,845m)

There's definitely something about Mary—this fearsome powder keg attracts Australia's finest boarders and skiers. They come here in order to try and tackle this brutal slope, in pride of place in Hotham's Extreme Zone.

Australia's skiing is sometimes dismissed as having verticals that are too small, snow cover that's too unpredictable, and slopes that are too gentle, but the country has one of the longest histories of downhill snowsports in the world. One of the claimants to the title of world's first ski club, the Kiandra Snow Shoe Club, was established here by Norwegian gold miners in 1861, and there are challenging slopes to be found if you take a closer look.

Although not the largest, Mount Hotham (or simply "Hotham" as it currently prefers to be called) is one of Australia's most popular ski resorts, and boasts the country's best annual average snowfall figures of about 10ft (3m) per year. Skiers have been making the 248-mile (400-km) trip here from Melbourne, and of course from further afield, for nearly a century now, since Hotham first gained notoriety for snow fun in the 1920s.

The Aussie freeriding experience

Unusually, Hotham is one of the few resorts in the world where the village is situated at the top of the mountain, with visitors skiing down to the bottom of the chairlift from their accommodation. Still more unusually, the most challenging terrain is on the lower, rather than the upper slopes—it's almost like your conventional ski resort in reverse, and all the more endearing for that. Thanks in part to that above-average snowfall record, but also its steeper-than-average terrain, with longer, steeper runs than the Aussie norm, it has built a freeriding reputation for skiers and boarders.

The most famous run here, and the one generally agreed to be the best, is Mary's Slide. Although it has only been lift-accessed since the late 1990s, the run was hike-to only for most of the last century, and its history goes back to the early years of the resort. The run is named after one of Hotham's early skiers and a three-times Australian ski champion, Mary Wallace (who later became Mary James), after she and three friends first skied it in 1938.

The story goes that Mary was a very accomplished, graceful skier and never fell over, but the three friends decided that this was the run where Mary would finally surpass the limits of her talent and take a tumble. In fact, the friends later admitted, she never did and they were just winding her up, but the name has stuck.

Today the Mary's Slide name has been expanded to cover a sector of the ski area in Hotham's "Extreme Zone," out past Heavenly Valley, and there are a variety of steep to very steep runs, including a wide-open powder bowl. However, the original trail remains the most challenging and is gate-accessed, then (depending on how the season has gone for snowfall) there may be a potentially large cornice to negotiate before the steep descent begins right down to the valley. For the maximum gradient, follow the ridge out to skier's left of the run rather than dropping straight in, then drop off down to skier's right where the run has already dropped way below you.

Mary's, like so many great runs and most of the less great ones, is best after a fresh powder dump, and happily Hotham gets more storms depositing 12in (30cm) or more overnight than most. The snow is usually dry and light, thanks to the long trip the precipitation makes from the ocean, most commonly arriving from the north. The southerly

LEFT: Going downhill fast on one of Australia's steepest slopes, but hopefully not going under. Skiing in Australia is an altogether different experience, starting with the famous warm Australian light and the bigger, deeper skies.

BELOW: Named after the lady who first skied it more than 75 years ago, but didn't slide, Mary's is widely acknowledged to be the most challenging slope in Australia. The run is at its steepest in the mid-section, and then careens speedily through the typical Hotham shrubs.

facing slopes then hold the snow—the reverse scenario to the benefits of north-facing runs in the northern hemisphere. Less happily, as it holds the reputation of "Australia's freeride capital," it means that you're likely to be in competition with other like-minded souls, and the earlier skier/boarder gets fresh tracks: late arrivals may find the run skied out. If there's less fresh powder, you're more likely to encounter vegetation and rocks peeking out through the snow. The vegetation grows into bush size, then becomes trees, on the lower half of the trail toward the bridge, which some rate as equally challenging to the steeps above.

Of course, although Mary's has the character, the history, and the snow to make it our Australian run of choice, debate rages on, as it should, as to which is Australia's toughest run. Mary's is in top spot there too for many, but others opt for descents such as Fanny's Finish at Mount Buller or even going right down to Tasmania to ski Rodway at Mount Mawson, where skiing west of the lift is the most challenging.

But back at Hotham, for insider tips on Mary's Slide (and other challenging runs such as Brockoff and Gotcha Ridge), double-black-diamond classes are organized twice daily by the resort, with workshop topics including skiing ice and very steep terrain. An excellent grounding.

Fact file Mary's Slide

IN SHORT: There's something about Mary

TOUGHNESS:
☠☠☠

FEAR FACTOR:
☠☠☠

VERTICAL: 1,296ft (395m)

AVERAGE TIME:
Anything between one and many minutes, depending on how many falls you take

LENGTH OF RUN:
0.9 miles (1.6km)

ACCESS: Chairlift

BEST TIME:
July–September

AVALANCHE KIT:
Nonessential

ALTITUDE RANGE: 4,756–6,052ft (1,450–1,845m)

SKIABLE AREA:
18.6 miles (30km)

RUNS: 63

LIFTS: 14

WEB: hotham.com.au

GETTING THERE:
Melbourne (223.2 miles/360km), Hotham airport (12.4 miles/20km)

AUSTRALIA

MOUNT HOTHAM
▲ 1,862m

MARY'S SLIDE
START
FINISH

Motatapu Chutes
Treble Cone, New Zealand
6,429ft (1,960m)

The Motatapu Chutes are known for their very steep, tight lines that leave you little room to maneuver, unlike anywhere else in the Southern Lakes.

Treble Cone has a reputation for some of the gnarliest terrain in the southern hemisphere and some of the most breathtaking scenery on the planet.

"TC," as it's sometimes known, can claim a number of New Zealand "best in shows," including having the country's biggest lift-served vertical at 2,296ft (700m), the greatest percentage of advanced or expert terrain at 45 percent, the biggest ski area on the South Island at 1,359 acres (550ha), and the largest recorded average annual snowfall at 216in (550cm), neatly matching that area measure.

Located around two hours' drive from Queenstown on the South Island, those spectacular views are out over Lake Wanaka and Mount Aspiring National Park. Wanaka is the local ski town, around 11.8 miles (19km) from the center's base area. The last 4.3 miles (7km) on the gravel access road up can be tricky, so be sure to carry chains.

But it's well worth the effort. The terrain sprawls across three vast basins with trails up to 2.6-miles (4.3-km) long. What used to be a 20-minute, lung-busting hike is now served by a fast, efficient lift system, including the country's first high-speed, six-seater chairlift.

Enter the double-black Motatapu Chutes
The best of the terrain for good skiers and boarders—both in-bounds and out—is accessed via the Saddle quad chairlift. Head to the left side (skier's right) of Saddle Basin and through the gate you'll enter the double-black-diamond Motatapu Chutes terrain.

"IT'S THE WAY IN FOR THE CONFIRMED ADRENALINE JUNKIE WISHING TO MINIMIZE THEIR TIME ON MORE GENTLE STUFF AND MAKE UP A MAXIMUM LAP COUNT."

218 | Motatapu Chutes, Treble Cone

LEFT: Treble Cone groom the trails every night—and if you catch the Saddle chairlift first thing in the morning, you'll get the honor of being the first to spoil these immaculate patterns.

FAR LEFT: The Motatapu Chutes are serious business and for expert skiers only. Even though some of the upper slopes are easy, make no mistake—the only way out is through the chutes themselves.

The Motatapu Chutes are long, wide, steep, and hopefully when you visit, powder filled. Gliding down from the top of the chair at Tim's Table, a fence runs the length of them with a choice of two access gates, open when conditions are right, one at the top and the other halfway down.

If you access by the upper gate, keep skier's right for the chutes or head down the comparatively mellow Hollywood Bowl—a wonderful, open powder bowl in its own right. There are around a dozen named chutes cut between a multitude of rocky outcrops and many more lines possible, including some very steep options for those in search of the most serious challenge. Expect narrow sections between rocky outcrops and plenty of bouncing off boulders and small (to rather large) cliff jumps.

The second gate takes you straight to the top of the more mellow side of the chutes without the gentler Meadows terrain above to cross, so it's the way in for the confirmed adrenaline junkie wishing to minimize their time on more gentle stuff and make up a maximum lap count. Treble Cone offers electronic ticketing that can track just how much vertical you clock up, as well as ski school classes in steep and deep. The routes around terrain features named "Diamond" and "The Fickle Finger of Fear" are among the best known lines, the latter easily accessed from the side of lower Hollywood Bowl. It progressively decreases in width to become a very narrow chute, in places little wider than a ski's length, so it is especially well named and a bit of a shock after the comparatively easy powder bowl above.

Avalanche kit essential

The Motatapu Chutes are patroled and only opened once conditions are good, avalanche-control work is complete, and they're deemed safe, but nonetheless it's wise to carry avalanche rescue equipment here (and to know how to use it).

Toward the bottom it's worth keeping in mind getting back to the base of the Saddle quad, with the rule being that the earlier you traverse and the further left you keep, the shorter the hike out. Indeed, set off early and there's no hike, just the traverse; stay right and your longest walk is going to be around 20 minutes up the prepared boot-packed track.

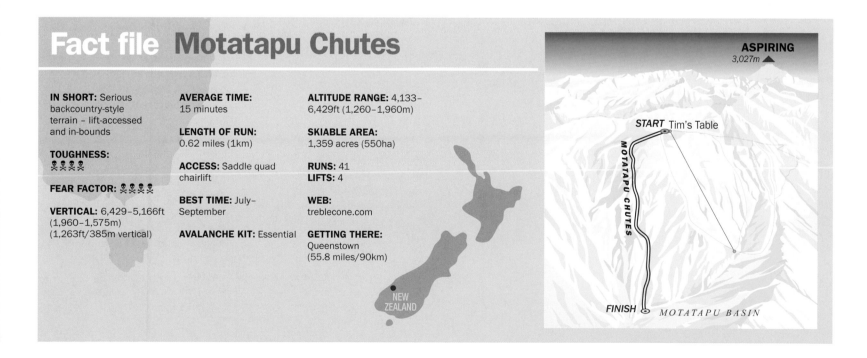

Fact file Motatapu Chutes

IN SHORT: Serious backcountry-style terrain – lift-accessed and in-bounds

TOUGHNESS:
☠☠☠☠

FEAR FACTOR: ☠☠☠☠

VERTICAL: 6,429–5,166ft (1,960–1,575m) (1,263ft/385m vertical)

AVERAGE TIME: 15 minutes

LENGTH OF RUN: 0.62 miles (1km)

ACCESS: Saddle quad chairlift

BEST TIME: July–September

AVALANCHE KIT: Essential

ALTITUDE RANGE: 4,133–6,429ft (1,260–1,960m)

SKIABLE AREA: 1,359 acres (550ha)

RUNS: 41

LIFTS: 4

WEB: treblecone.com

GETTING THERE: Queenstown (55.8 miles/90km)

NEW ZEALAND

ASPIRING
3,027m ▲

START Tim's Table

MOTATAPU CHUTES

FINISH — MOTATAPU BASIN

Index

The author

PATRICK THORNE—also known as "The Snow Hunter"—has been a writer all his life, publishing his first skiing book in 1985. He worked as a journalist and editor on *Skier* magazine in London in the mid-1980s before setting out on a personal quest in 1992 to locate every ski area on the planet, a task never before attempted.

Patrick went on to build a database of all the ski areas in the world, eventually hunting down more than 6,000 areas in 80 countries—a database that today sits behind many of the world's ski information sites, books, and brochures.

Over the years Patrick has gained a formidable worldwide client list ranging from Microsoft, Berlitz, Rough Guides, AOL, the BBC, and Teletext in the 1990s through to Virgin, Skiinfo, Frommers, Nokia, and Burton more recently. As well as writing for publications worldwide, Patrick has been featured in many of them himself. His work has also been sold to top resorts around the world, including Aspen, Intrawest, Madonna di Campiglio, Sun Valley, Verbier, and Zermatt. Patrick is currently editor of *InTheSnow* magazine.

Foreword

Austrian **AXEL NAGLICH** skis mountains that no one has dared before. In the last few years Axel pioneered some of the most extreme ski routes around the globe. He skied the slopes of Nuptse in the Himalayas, broke new trails in South America, skied down Mount Elbrus (Europe's highest Peak), and left his mark on Iran's Mount Damavand.

In 2007, Axel was part of an expedition to the remote Mount St. Elias in Alaska to ski the longest snow covered vertical line on the planet.

His vision not only became a reality, but also an epic, awe-inspiring motion picture, simply entitled *Mount St. Elias*—the portrait of a mountain and its conquerors.

Author acknowledgments

Kees Albers, Ekkehard Assmann, Johannes Badrutt, Frank Baldwin, Jackie Barclay, Jane Bolton, Jon Brooke, Simon Calder, Richard Davidson, Vic Delstanche, Lynsey Devon, Chris Exall, Debbie Gabriel, Sarah Greaney, Vanessa Green, Rachel Gunnells, Alison and Phil Heyworth, Becky Horton, Alan and Sarah Hunt, Dominic Killinger, Richard Leafe, Sarah Lewis, Ivo Marloh, Rupert Mellor, Julie Merie, Sondre Norheim, Steven, Susan and Matthew Ogston, Dave Pellatt, Jimmy Petterson, Heidi Reisz, Ben Ross, Hannes Schneider, Xavier Schouller, Espen Schroder, Christoph Schrahe, Chris and Gail Surtees, Geoff Sutton, Marion Telsnig, Alexander, Catherine, Derek, Robert, Sally and Sam Thorne, Keith Tilson, David Tordoff, John and Penny Whiting, Arnie Wilson, Stephen Wilkinson, Paul Wisely, Stephen Wood, Duncan Worrell and Mathias Zdarsky.

(Squaw Valley) Amelia Richmond; (Heavenly) Roger Ainger, May Lilley, Russ Pecoraro; (Snowbasin) Brooke Broderick, Jason Dyer; (Jackson Hole) Danica Celix, Anna Olson, Eric Seymour; (Aspen Snowmass) Richard E. Burkley, Lindsy Fortier, Matthew Hamilton, Jeff Hanle, Gabriella Le Breton, Tim Mutrie, Steve Sewell, Lea Tucker; (Stowe) Jeff Wise; (Jackson Hole) Danica Celix; (Whistler Blackcomb) Jill Young; (Revelstoke) Ashley Tait, Sarah Windsor; (Lake Louise) Sandy Best, Chris Davenport, Alison Jones, Charlie Locke, Robin Locke, Dan Markham; (Mont-Sainte-Anne) Lisa Marie Lacasse, Amélie Leclerc; Hugues Leclerc; (Kangaamiut) Hans Solmssen; (Lyngen Lodge) Graham Austick; (Åre) Pernilla Enqvist, Elisabeth Hallbäck, Linda Wasell; (Nevis Range) Heather Negus, Elma McMenemy, Jeff Starkey; (Baqueiera Beret) Josi Martinez, Roberto Buil and Xavier Ubeira; (Pic du Midi) Laurence de Boerio, Claude Etchelecou, Vanessa Fisher; (La Plagne) Anaïs Alaurent, Mika Bishop, Séverine Gonthier, Jo Lowe, Snow Crazy Chris; (Alpe d'Huez) Kevan Barber, Clémentine, Celine Perrillon; (Val d'Isère) Jane Jaquemod; (Les Arcs) Stephanie Briggs, Julie Merle, Snow Crazy Chris; (Chamonix) Claire Burnet; (Mittenwald) Melanie Gilhaus; (St Anton am Arlberg) Pia Herbst, Miriam Scherl; (Igls, Innsbruck) Catrin Haas, Eric Wolf; (Dachstein) Christoph Buchegger, Marlene Scheidl; (Stubai) Alexandra Reinisch; (Mürren) Vanessa Fisher; (Verbier) Hans Solmssen; (Engadin) Michael Anrig, Stéphanie Emer, Sara Roloff, Angela Rupp, Stefan Wyss; (Portes du Soleil) Cosima Page, Antoine Schaller; (Davos Klosters) Aurelia Schmid; (Zermatt Cervinia) Dominique Fabian Mauderli, Janine Imesch; (Cortina d'Ampezzo) Sue Freeman, Marianne Moretti; (Alta Badia) Nicole Dorigo; (Etna) Nino Lo Giudice; (Kanin Sella Nevea) Tina Batistuta; (Nepal) Craig Calonica; (Portillo) Rebecca Armstrong; (Las Leñas) Mark Lasseter; (Hotham) Gina Woodward; (New Zealand): Michael Steven.

Picture credits

The editors and publisher gratefully acknowledge permission to use copyright material in this book. Copyright holders are acknowledged on this page with their individual copyright item. Every effort has been made to trace and contact copyright holders. If there are any inadvertent omissions or if credits have been wrongly attributed we apologize to those concerned, and ask that you contact us so that we can correct any oversight in the next edition. The contact details are given on the next page.

1 © Andre Schoenherr/Stubaier Gletscherbahn; 2–3 © Alaska Stock/Alamy; 8–9 © Andre Schoenherr/Stubaier Gletscherbahn; 10–11; © Seth K. Hughes/Alamy; 12–13 © Aurora Photos/Alamy; 14 © SCPhotos/Alamy; 15 SCPhotos/Alamy; 16–17 © Corey Rich; 17 © Heavenly Mountain Resort; 18 © H. Mark Weidman Photography/Alamy; 21 © Snowbasin Resort; 22–23 © Stephen Saks Photography/Alamy; 24–25 © Jackson Hole Mountain Resort; 26–27 © Jackson Hole Mountain Resort; 29 © Aspen Skiing Company; 30 © Greg Petrics/Stowe Mountain Resort; 31 © Marshall Ikonography/Alamy; 32 © Greg Petrics/Stowe Mountain Resort; 33 (top) Scott Braaten/Stowe Mountain Resort; (bottom) © Greg Petrics/Stowe Mountain Resort; 34–35 © Vitek Ludvik/Red Bull Content Pool; 36 © Vitek Ludvik/Red Bull Content Pool; 37 © Volker Holzner/Red Bull Content Pool; 38–39 © Vitek Ludvik/Red Bull Content Pool; 40 © Reed Purvis/Alamy; 41 © All Canada Photos/Alamy; 42 © Randy Lincks/Alamy; 44 © All Canada Photos/Alamy; 46 © Aurora Photos/Alamy; 47 © Revelstoke Mountain Resort; 48 © Paul Zizka Photography; 49 © Lake Louise Ski Resort; 50–51 © Paul Zizka Photography; 52–53 © Andre Olivier Lyra/Mont-Sainte-Anne Resort; 54 © Hemis/Alamy; 55 © Andre Olivier Lyra/Mont-Sainte-Anne Resort; 56–57 © Graham Austick/Lyngen Lodge; 58–59 © Hans Solmssen; 60 © Hans Solmssen; 62–63 © Graham Austick/Lyngen Lodge; 64 (top) © Graham Austick/Skiing Lyngen 64 (bottom) © Graham Austick/Skiing Lyngen; 65 © Graham Austick/Skiing Lyngen; 66 © Fleur Maxwell-Middle; 67 © Jonas Kullman/SkiStar; 68–69 © Steven McKenna/ski-scotland; 71 © Nevis Range; 72–73 © ROYER Philippe/SAGAPHOTO.COM/Alamy; 74–75 © Baqueria Beret Ski Resort; 76 © Baqueria Beret Ski Resort; 77 © Baqueira Beret Tourist Office; 79 © Hemis/Alamy; 80 © Cedric Bernardini/cedricbernardini.com; 81 © Pic Du Midi; 83 © P Royer and Office de Promotion de la Grande Plagne; 84–85 © P Royer and Office de Promotion de la Grande Plagne; 86–87 © Laurent Salino/Alpe d'Huez Tourisme; 88–89 ©Alpe d'Huez Tourisme; 90–91 © Laurent Salino/Alpe D'Huez Tourisme; 92 © Jp. Noisillier/Agence Nuts.fr; 92–93 © Emma Wood/Alamy; 94–95 © Pete Webb/Paradiski; 96 © StfW/Alamy; 97 © ROYER Philippe/SAGAPHOTO.COM/Alamy; 98 © Chris Mellor; 100–101 © Aurora Photos/Alamy; 101 © SuperStock/Alamy; 102–103 © dpa picture alliance/Alamy; 104 © epa european pressphoto agency b.v./Alamy; 105 © Bernd Brägelmann; 106 © LOOK Die Bildagentur der Fotografen GmbH/Alamy; 107 © Peter Lehner/Mittenwald Tourist Office; 108–109 © Westend61 GmbH/Alamy; 110

© LOOK Die Bildagentur der Fotografen GmbH/Alamy; 110–111 © St Anton Tourist Office; 114 © Ben Fillmore/Alamy; 114–115 © LOOK Die Bildagentur der Fotografen GmbH/Alamy; 116 © Prisma Bildagentur AG/Alamy; 118–119 © skisport.com; 120 © Westend61 GmbH/Alamy; 122–123 © Georg Krewenka (krewenka.com); 124 © Georg Krewenka (krewenka.com); 125 © Georg Krewenka (krewenka.com); 126–127 © Andre Schoenherr/Stubaier Gletscherbahn; 128–129 © Andre Schoenherr/Stubaier Gletscherbahn; 130–131 © Andre Schoenherr/Stubaier Gletscherbahn; 132–133 © Bart Pro/Alamy; 134 © photostaud/Alamy; 135 (top left) © Paul Painter/Alamy; 135 (top right) © Paul Painter/Alamy; 137 © Terje Sannum; 138–139 © Robert Fried/Alamy; 141 © Engadin St Moritz Mountains – Bosch; 142 © StockShot/Alamy; 144–145 © Extreme Sports Photo/Alamy; 146–147 © Destination Davos Klosters; 148 © Howard Brundrett/Alamy; 149 © Whit Richardson/Alamy; 150–151 © blickwinkel/Alamy; 152 © The Aosta Valley Tourist Office; 153 © The Aosta Valley Tourist Office; 154–155 © Bandion.it/Cortina d'Ampezzo Tourist Office; 156 © Dino Colli/Cortina d'Ampezzo Tourist Office; 157 © Paola Dandrea/Cortina d'Ampezzo Tourist Office; 158–159 © Erik Dilexit www.erikdilexit.com; 160 © Alpine Logistics; 162–163 © Alta Badia Tourist Office; 164 © Alta Badia Tourist Office; 165 © Alta Badia Tourist Office; 166 © Glyn Thomas Photography/Alamy; 168–169 © CuboImages srl/Alamy; 170–171 © Tomas Jancik/Alamy; 172–173 © Jan Remmelg/verticalwayaround.com; 174 © Vino Anthony/ chrisanthony.com; 175 © All Canada Photos/Alamy; 176–177 © Adam Radosavljevic: Poland/Alamy; 178 © maciej czajka/Alamy; 179 © Hayden Richard Verry/Alamy; 180 © Crispian Wilson/Alamy; 181 © Latasha Estelle Wilson/takingteainturkey.com; 182 © Dikoz/Shutterstock; 184–185 © Chris Luthy/Crystalski.co.uk; 186 © Mark Meadows; 187 © Corbis; 188–189 © Craig Calonica heliskinepal.com; 190 © PhotosIndia.com RM 9/Alamy; 191 © Graham Crouch/Alamy; 192 (top) © Angus Blount Greene; 192 (bottom) © Fran McElhone; 194–195 © Craig Calonica heliskinepal.com; 196 © International Photobank/Alamy; 197 © Craig Calonica heliskinepal.com; 200–201 © Mark Lasseter/southamericaski.com; 202–203 © Ski Portillo/Rogier van Rijn; 205 © Ski Portillo/Adam Clark; 206 © Ski Portillo; 208–209 © Mark Lasseter of SouthAmericaSki.com; 210 © Mark Lasseter of SouthAmericaSki.com; 211 © Mark Lasseter of SouthAmericaSki.com; 212–213 © Mount Hotham Alpine Resort; 214 © Mount Hotham Alpine Resort; 215 © Mount Hotham Alpine Resort; 216–217 © Treble Cone Ski Area; 218 © Treble Cone Ski Area; 219 © Treble Cone Ski Area.

All maps and illustrations by Mark Franklin: markfranklinarts.co.uk

Carmelite House
50 Victoria Embankment
London
EC4Y oDZ

First published in 2014

A catalogue record of this book is available from the British Library

ISBN 978 1 84866 387 9

Printed and bound in China

10